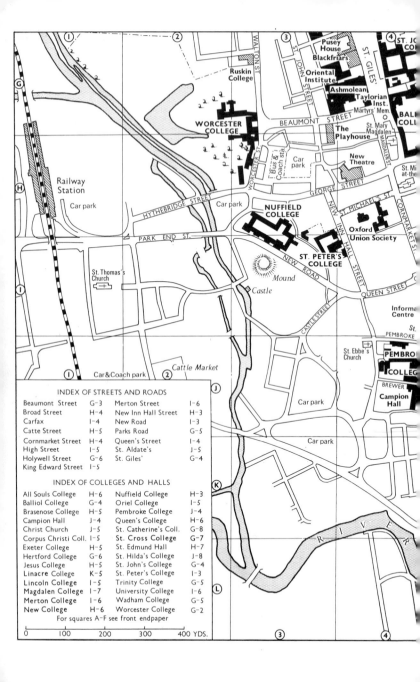

INDEX OF STREETS AND ROADS

Beaumont Street	G-3	Merton Street	I-6
Broad Street	H-4	New Inn Hall Street	H-3
Carfax	I-4	New Road	I-3
Catte Street	H-5	Parks Road	G-5
Cornmarket Street	H-4	Queen's Street	I-4
High Street	I-5	St. Aldate's	J-5
Holywell Street	G-6	St. Giles'	G-4
King Edward Street	I-5		

INDEX OF COLLEGES AND HALLS

All Souls College	H-6	Nuffield College	H-3
Balliol College	G-4	Oriel College	I-5
Brasenose College	H-5	Pembroke College	J-4
Campion Hall	J-4	Queen's College	H-6
Christ Church	J-5	St. Catherine's Coll.	G-8
Corpus Christi Coll.	I-5	St. Cross College	G-7
Exeter College	H-5	St. Edmund Hall	H-7
Hertford College	G-6	St. Hilda's College	J-8
Jesus College	H-5	St. John's College	G-4
Linacre College	K-5	St. Peter's College	I-3
Lincoln College	I-5	Trinity College	G-5
Magdalen College	I-7	University College	I-6
Merton College	I-6	Wadham College	G-5
New College	H-6	Worcester College	G-2
	For squares A-F see front endpaper		

0   100   200   300   400 YDS.

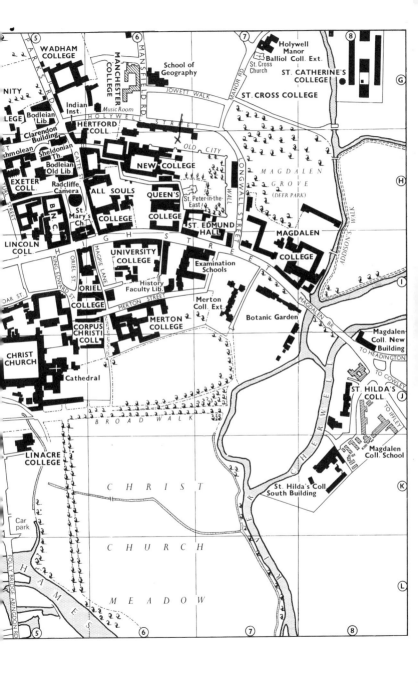

THE
CLARENDON GUIDE TO
OXFORD

BY

A. R. WOOLLEY

SECOND EDITION

OXFORD UNIVERSITY PRESS
1972

Oxford University Press, Ely House, London W.1

GLASGOW   NEW YORK   TORONTO   MELBOURNE   WELLINGTON
CAPE TOWN   IBADAN   NAIROBI   DAR ES SALAAM   LUSAKA   ADDIS ABABA
DELHI   BOMBAY   CALCUTTA   MADRAS   KARACHI   LAHORE   DACCA
KUALA LUMPUR   SINGAPORE   HONG KONG   TOKYO

FIRST EDITION 1963
SECOND EDITION 1972

PRINTED IN GREAT BRITAIN
AT THE UNIVERSITY PRESS, OXFORD
BY VIVIAN RIDLER
PRINTER TO THE UNIVERSITY

PREFACE

IN June 1915 the late C. R. L. Fletcher wrote *A Handy Guide to Oxford* for the benefit of those wounded soldiers in the Third Southern General Hospital who were sufficiently recovered to start exploring the beautiful city to which their wounds had brought them. The main part of the hospital was in the Examination Schools and he described short walks, beginning with his own college of Magdalen and extending to the whole of the University and colleges.

Fletcher's style was at once scholarly, whimsical, humorous, and his book was reprinted many times until 1946, when it had become out of date and also ran out of print.

This new *Clarendon Guide* is intended to replace it, but it owes nothing in plan or design to its predecessor, the genius of which is inimitable. Moreover, many books about Oxford have appeared in the last fifty years and I am deeply indebted to them. There are two upon which I have especially depended. They are the volume on the City of Oxford by the Royal Commission on Historical Monuments of England, published in 1939, and that on the University of Oxford which forms Volume III in the *Victoria History of the County of Oxford*, 1954. The best account of the origin and early history of the University is to be found in Volume III of the late Hastings Rashdall's *The Universities of Europe in the Middle Ages*, edited by F. M. Powicke and A. B. Emden, 1936.

Guides to living and growing institutions soon become out of date; new buildings rise apace, the number of University students varies, times at which colleges are open to visitors may alter. But the core of Oxford has kept its present character for centuries and it is hoped that the present book, brought up to date as opportunity offers, will retain its usefulness for many years.

My thanks are particularly due to Dr. A. B. Emden, F.B.A., late Principal of St. Edmund Hall, and to Dr. W. A. Pantin, F.B.A., formerly Keeper of the Archives and Fellow of Oriel, who know more about Oxford than anybody else, for kindly reading the typescript and making many corrections and suggestions. Many others, especially at the University Press, have also helped and such mistakes as have survived are my own. The photographs are reproduced by courtesy of Thomas-Photos., Oxford. Mr. C. J. Danby, Fellow of Worcester, has kindly checked and corrected all the information about the science laboratories and their work.

In the list of the more famous members of the various colleges a difference may be noticed between those of the men's colleges and the women's: the reason is the simple one that, for the most part, the men's colleges have a much longer history and therefore far more claimants to inclusion.

NOTE. The number of Fellows, scholars, and commoners prefixed to the accounts of the several colleges is taken from the *University Calendar* for 1971.

CONTENTS

TIMES OF OPENING TO THE PUBLIC   vii

INTRODUCTION   I

A CONDUCTED TOUR   14

PLACES OF INTEREST NEAR OXFORD   149

SOME BOOKS ABOUT OXFORD   150

INDEX   152

TIMES OF OPENING TO THE PUBLIC

COLLEGES

ALL SOULS	2-5.
BALLIOL	10.30-5.
BRASENOSE	10-6 (earlier in winter) in term; 9 till dusk in vacation.
CHRIST CHURCH	Cathedral: all day till Evensong at 6; quadrangles: 9-4.30; hall and library: occasionally in the afternoon; picture gallery: 2-4.30 on weekdays; Christ Church Meadow: 7-dusk.
CORPUS CHRISTI	1.30-4 on week-days in term; 10-4 on Sundays and in vacation (but 10-6 in Long Vacation and on Sundays in Trinity Term).
EXETER	9 till dusk. Fellows' garden: 2-4.
HERTFORD	Chapel: afternoon (no set times).
JESUS	10-4.
KEBLE	All day. Chapel: 10-4.30 on week-days.
LINCOLN	2-5 on week-days; 11-5 on Sundays.
MAGDALEN	2-6.15 on week-days; 10-6.15 on Sundays; 1 July-15 September: 10-7 daily.
MANCHESTER	Chapel: all day.
MERTON	10-4.30 (4 in winter). Library: 10-12 and 2-4.30 (4 in winter) on week-days.
NEW COLLEGE	2-5 Monday-Friday; 12-6 Saturday and Sunday.
NUFFIELD	All day.
ORIEL	2-5 in term; 10-6 in Long Vacation.
PEMBROKE	9-6 (or dusk).
QUEEN'S	2-4 in term; 10-6 (5 in winter) in vacation.
ST. CATHERINE'S	All day.
ST. EDMUND HALL	During daylight.
ST. JOHN'S	1 (10 in vacation)-7 (5 in winter) on week-days; 10-1 on Sunday.
ST. PETER'S	Chapel: all day in term only.
TRINITY	2-7 (dusk in winter).

UNIVERSITY	2–4 in term; 10–7 (earlier in winter) in vacation.
WADHAM	11–5.
WORCESTER	2–6 (dusk in winter) in term and vacation; also 9–12 in vacation.

UNIVERSITY INSTITUTIONS, ETC.

Ashmolean Museum	10–4; Sundays 2–4.
Bodleian Library	Monday–Friday 9–5; Saturday 9–12.30.
Botanic Garden	1 October–31 March: 9–4.30 on week-days; 10–12, 2–4.30 on Sundays. 1 April–30 September: 8–5 on week-days; 10–12, 2–6 on Sundays. Green-houses 2–4 daily.
Convocation House Divinity School	Monday–Friday 9–5; Saturday 9–12.
Examination Schools	Usually 2.15–4.30 (4 in vacation) on week-days.
Museum of the History of Science, Old Ashmolean	10.30–1 and 2.30–4 on week-days (except Saturday afternoons).
Pitt Rivers Museum (Ethnology, &c.)	10–1 and 1–4 on week-days.
Sheldonian Theatre	10–1 and 2–5 (4 in winter) on week-days.
The Painted Room (3 Cornmarket)	10.30–12.30 and 2.30–4.30 on Monday–Friday.
University Church of St. Mary the Virgin	7 till dusk.
University Museum (Parks Road)	10–4 on week-days.

It can be assumed that buildings not listed here are not normally open to the public.

All the times of opening listed above are subject to alteration.

INTRODUCTION

OXFORD is one of the greatest architectural treasuries of the world. It contains examples of every building style in England from the eleventh century to the twentieth and they are good examples. Not only are they buildings which for the most part have been the objects of the care, devotion, and pride of those for whom they were built, but at no point in history was Oxford devastated by war or revolution, though numerous and splendid monastic and conventual structures disappeared at the Reformation when the religious houses were dissolved. Architecturally Oxford has never ceased to be alive, every age producing its own fashion and answering its problem in its own idiom. The result has been that unique concentration within an area of less than half a square mile of towers, pinnacles, and domes described in Arnold's happy phrase as 'that sweet city with her dreaming spires [that] needs not June for beauty's heightening'. No place in the world looks more like the 'celestial city' than does Oxford seen from Boars Hill in the light of the evening sun or from the hill at Elsfield in the morning.

Furthermore, Oxford shares with Cambridge the distinction of being the seat of one of the two universities in Europe which have preserved the medieval collegiate system, a system not always readily understood by the visitor who may get confused about the difference between the colleges and the University. It is hoped to make this difference clear in the following pages.

As a town Oxford is nothing like so old as London or York, Canterbury, Lincoln, or Cambridge. It has no Roman or British origin. St. Frideswide's Priory, the church of which is now the Cathedral of the diocese of Oxford, was probably founded early in the eighth century, but the first time Oxford comes into written history is with a mention in the *Anglo-Saxon Chronicle* under the year 911, when it passed from Mercia into the hands of Edward, King of the

West Saxons. It began as a frontier town on the Thames, built for protection against the Danes. It became an important road junction and river-crossing, the most central of English midland towns. Militarily it was well protected, for it stood at the end of a long gravel promontory, surrounded on three sides by rivers and water-meadows liable to flood.

Oxford rapidly came into prominence as the meeting-place of national councils. Edmund Ironside died here in 1017 and Harold Harefoot in 1040. Under William the Conqueror it was fortified with a castle, within the bailey of which there was erected a collegiate chapel dedicated to St. George, one of the earliest known dedications to England's patron saint: of these there still stand the Mound and the tower and crypt of St. George's. Of the churches which graced the city in Norman times there are still to be seen the Saxon tower of St. Michael-at-the-North-Gate (*c.* 1000), the crypt and chancel of St. Peter-in-the-East (*c.* 1140), and the greater part of the monastic church of St. Frideswide, now the Cathedral. Iffley Church, which stands just over a mile down the Thames, dates from about 1180, an almost perfect example of a late Norman parish church.

Whatever may be thought of the climate of Oxford in these days, it recommended itself to the men of the Middle Ages who frequently extolled it in prose and verse. Henry I (1100–35) built himself a residence close to where the Ashmolean Museum now stands and his grandson, Henry II (1154–89) was fond of staying there—indeed, Richard Cœur de Lion and probably also King John were born in Oxford at this Beaumont Palace. It was later given by Edward III to the Carmelites whose residence there is now commemorated only by the name of a passage called Friars' Entry.

No one knows when the University began. It had no founder, but was a spontaneous growth answering to that stir of intellectual life which had recently produced the older universities of Bologna and Paris, and the relationship between Oxford and Paris was close for the first two centuries of their growth. We do, however, know something of the Oxford in which the scholars began to congregate. Robert

2

d'Oilly, to whom William the Conqueror had entrusted the Castle, founded therein the College of the Secular Canons of St. George and these became a learned body. Close neighbours were the Augustinian foundations of St. Frideswic 's Priory and Oseney Abbey (founded 1129), and there was the royal residence just mentioned.

From 1096 till 1102, and possibly later, Theobald of Étampes lectured and called himself a Master of Oxford: in 1133 Robert Pullen lectured on the Scriptures; perhaps as early as 1149 an Italian, Vacarius, lectured on Roman Law. In 1167 the quarrel between Henry II and Philip Augustus closed the University of Paris to Englishmen and thus probably stimulated Oxford to take shape as a full *studium generale* or 'university'. At any rate, from this point its development was rapid and Gerald of Wales, lecturing about 1186, claimed a large audience of doctors, masters, and scholars. The names are known of several scholars who studied at Oxford before 1200, one of the most notable being St. Edmund of Abingdon. Thus there was by the turn of the century a body of scholars organized on the lines of the University of Paris. The course usually began when the student was about sixteen years of age and lasted, like other apprenticeships, for seven years. It embraced the Seven Liberal Arts, the *Trivium* (Grammar, Rhetoric, Logic—i.e. the correct modes of expression of thought) and the *Quadrivium* (Arithmetic, Geometry, Astronomy, Music); to these were soon added Natural, Moral, and Metaphysical Philosophy. The first degree was that of Bachelor of Arts (B.A.), taken after four years, and the Master's or M.A. degree was in effect a licence to teach in any university in Europe.

Examination was by public disputation and argument—writing material was scarce and too expensive for such a purpose. For the first few years after incepting, i.e. beginning as Masters, M.A.s were *Regent Masters*, teaching and examining in the schools of the University. There were also courses of study for degrees (Bachelor and Doctor) in the higher faculties of Theology, Law, or Medicine, which many pursued. All members of the University were in at least Minor Orders of the Church and were subject to

3

ecclesiastical law. The academic robes still worn are a permanent reminder of this status.

Where did these masters and scholars live, teach, and learn? At first they lived in lodgings and hired houses where they were subject to overcharging, cheating, and ill treatment, which were often the consequence of, and were often repaid by, ill-disciplined and riotous behaviour. It is never easy to control young men: it must have been incredibly difficult when they were scattered throughout the streets and lanes of an intricate medieval town. The situation led inevitably to a great deal of ill-feeling, the sort of feeling that arises when alien troops are billeted, and every few years it boiled up into bloody affrays. One of the first and most momentous of the disputes, though not a particularly bloody one, arose in 1209. A woman of the town was killed accidentally, so it was said, by scholars. The Mayor and burgesses raided the lodgings of the alleged culprits, who had fled, and seized hostages. The country at the time was under Interdict owing to the quarrel between Pope Innocent III and King John, who gave the townsmen leave to execute their prisoners. The University took alarm and dispersed, some to Reading, some to Paris, and some to Cambridge, where the sister university thus began. Not until 1213 did John give in to the Pope and the town to the Papal Legate, from whom the University received the earliest charter still in its possession. It provided the first university endowment, the townsmen being required to pay to the University fifty-two shillings a year in perpetuity, and for the next ten years house and room rents were to be half what they had been. After that rents of new *hospitia* were to be assessed by four Masters of Arts and four townsmen, known as Taxors. The annual fine was soon shouldered by the monks of Eynsham and since the monasteries were dissolved in 1536–9 it has been paid by the Chancellor of the Exchequer.

In the long struggle between town and University, the streets were often the scene of strife. The bells of St. Martin at Carfax rallied the citizens to battle and the bells of St. Mary the Virgin summoned the scholars. But the University, backed as a rule by Church and King, was emphatically the victor. After the great battle of St. Scholastica's Day, 10 February 1355, the Chancellor of the University with his officers, the two Proctors, the Taxors, and the Clerks of the Market controlled the quality of bread and ale, checked weights and measures, fixed rents, exercised discipline over citizen and scholar alike in the streets, whose cleansing they also supervised. Mayor and Sheriffs, on admission to office, swore to respect the privileges of the University and, indeed, on every 10 February from 1357 till 1825 the Mayor, Bailiffs, and sixty burgesses had to attend a service of penance at St. Mary's and offer one penny each upon the altar to atone for the scholars slain in the riots. Only in 1856 was an Act passed repealing the obligation imposed on the Mayor by 'His late Majesty King Henry III' (1216–72) to swear to preserve the liberties of the University.[1]

It is a testimony to the reputation of Oxford early in the thirteenth century that the Dominican friars set up their chief house of studies there on their arrival in England in 1221. Three years later the Franciscans did likewise. The conventual buildings of both, with their great churches, not a trace of which remains, were set up in the parish of St. Ebbe's, round Paradise Square, Friars' Street, and Littlegate Street.

The first known Chancellor of the University was Robert Grosseteste, one of the greatest scholars and churchmen in English history, who became Rector of the Oxford Franciscans in 1224 and Bishop of Lincoln in 1235. Since his day there has been an unbroken succession of Chancellors and their names are known. At first the Chancellor was responsible to the Bishop of Lincoln whose officer he was, but the University soon became self-governing. Its officers, besides the Chancellor, were the two Proctors, and the Taxors, and the Clerks of the Market, whose business lay largely with the townsmen. The governing body of the University was the whole number of resident Masters and Doctors, called Congregation.

For many years the University had no buildings or

[1] C. E. Mallet, *A History of the University of Oxford*, iii. 331, n.

property of its own. Congregation met in the Church of St. Mary the Virgin, which soon became the University Church, and the Faculty of Arts in St. Mildred's, a church which stood where Lincoln College now is. Lectures were given in hired 'schools' and the scholars lived a precarious life with the townsmen. Gradually the picture changed. To the first endowment in 1214, already mentioned, were added many others: for instance in 1243 a certain Alan Basset bequeathed eight marks a year ($8 \times 13s. 4d. = 8 \times 67p$) for two scholars to be chosen by Bicester Priory, and Ela, Countess of Warwick, whose memorial is in the Cathedral, gave 120 marks in 1293. Benefactions like these continued till the end of the fifteenth century. Chests were made to hold both the money and the pledges against which money was lent to Masters and scholars. Each chest had several locks and various officials held the keys.

An endowment of a somewhat different kind came in 1249 when William of Durham left 310 marks for twelve M.A.s to study Theology. Unfortunately the University was not experienced in managing such gifts, and though land was bought, much of the money was lost and not till between 1280 and 1292 was there a hall set up in which four Masters could live and study for the Doctorate in Divinity. In due time this hall developed into University College, which claims and was accorded the first place in the *University Calendar* until Colleges were put into alphabetical order in 1970.

Meanwhile, *c.* 1263, John de Balliol, also from County Durham, was enjoined as a penance to provide for the maintenance of scholars in Oxford. He died soon after, but his widow, Dervorguilla, carried out the intention and by 1282 Balliol College had come into existence on part of the site which it still occupies. In 1264 Walter de Merton, Chancellor of England and Bishop of Rochester, having acquired lands in Oxford and Cambridge because he was not yet sure which he would choose, devoted a great part of his fortune in landed property to the foundation and endowment of Merton College. The statutes he devised are not only still preserved in their beautiful writing in Merton's treasury, but they became the model for all subsequent collegiate foundations in both the English universities.

In 1280 the Cistercian monks built Rewley Abbey as a house to which they could send their members to study in Oxford, and in 1283 Sir John Giffard gave land and tenements, where Worcester College now is, as a place to which at first St. Peter's, Gloucester, and later also other Benedictine abbeys in the province of Canterbury could send their monks. From *c.* 1290 the monks of Durham also had a house in Oxford and some of its buildings are now a part of Trinity College.

When, in 1320, Thomas Cobham, Bishop of Worcester, built a Congregation House and library over it alongside the chancel of St. Mary the Virgin's, the University acquired its first real property, and thenceforward the likelihood of migration whether to Cambridge or to Northampton or Stamford was much reduced. Even so, in 1334, after a quarrel between the 'Nations', some of the northerners, students from Scotland and England north of the Nene, went to Stamford whence they had to return by order of the King (the other 'Nation' included men from south of the Nene, the Welsh, and the Irish).[1] The threat of secession was sufficiently dangerous for an oath to be required of everyone on his inception as M.A. that he would not lecture at Stamford, and this continued till 1827. In 1439 Abbot Hokenorton of Oseney built for the use of the Faculty of Arts the first lecture rooms or 'Schools', somewhere near where the north-west part of the Old Schools quadrangle now stands. In this area are still grouped the principal University buildings.

Though colleges continued to be founded at intervals, Exeter in 1314, Oriel in 1326, Queen's in 1341, and New College in 1379, the bulk of the student body, particularly the undergraduate part of it, went on living scattered about the town; but in the interests of discipline and security most became members of halls or *hospitia* (sometimes also called *inns* or *entries*). The heads of these were Principals, who

[1] 'Northerners' included men from the Diocese of Lichfield, Coventry, and Chester and the northern half of the Diocese of Lincoln.

normally had to be graduates of the University and who were licensed annually by the Chancellor. The names and sites of 120 of these halls are known though probably not more than eighty flourished at any one time. Many belonged to local religious houses, particularly to Oseney Abbey and St. John's Hospital, and some to colleges which rented them to successive Principals. They had their ups and downs in accordance with the character and reputation of their Principals, but their real weakness was that, unlike the colleges, they had no landed property, no endowments and, therefore, no permanent corporate existence. Thus when the colleges, after *c.* 1500, opened their doors to undergraduates as well as graduates, and to the sons of noblemen and gentry, who paid for what they got, as well as to the clever boys (scholars), who were 'on the foundation', the halls went into a rapid decline. In 1450 there were still fifty halls and only ten colleges, excluding those for monks and friars. In 1500 the number of halls had dropped to twenty-five and by 1558 there were only seven or eight,[1] but the number of colleges had increased to fifteen and they had grown much both in wealth and splendour. Repeated attempts were made during the fifteenth century to eliminate the solitary student living in lodgings, and indeed in 1400 a statute was passed requiring all students to live either in colleges or halls. Long before that it had been necessary for every student to have his name on the roll (*matricula*) of some Master who was responsible for his studies. In effect this continues today and every undergraduate member of the University must be presented initially for matriculation by one of the colleges or halls. They have power to accept or reject whom they will, but in practice there would be no point in accepting anyone who was unable to satisfy the minimum examination requirements of the University.

This brief introduction will have achieved its purpose if it has made clear the distinction between the University and the colleges and halls. The University came first and the

---

[1] *The Victoria County History of Oxfordshire* gives 70 halls in 1450; 60 in 1470; 56 in 1500, and 12 in 1543. See A. B. Emden, *An Oxford Hall in Medieval Times* (Oxford, 1927).

colleges and halls grew up in answer to the need of scholars to study in peace and quiet and, in the case of the colleges, to furnish able scholars with the financial means of pursuing their studies for the M.A. and higher degrees. In a sense every college, with its gate-tower and battlements, its hall (or refectory), kitchen, brewery, chapel, library, was a self-contained fortress set in the midst of a population frequently hostile. Usually college founders were wealthy men who assigned landed estates for the upkeep of their beneficiaries but not all colleges are equally well endowed: some are poor.[1] All the older ones have their rent rolls and bursars' accounts as well as their title-deeds in their muniment rooms and these commonly date back to the year of foundation. Even the first colleges, Merton, Balliol, University, still possess their foundation charters and first statutes. All of them are independent legal personalities, incorporated by royal charter.

The governing body of a college consists of its Head (variously named) and Fellows. The Head is elected by the Fellows until retiring age (except that the Crown appoints the Dean of Christ Church for life). New Fellows are elected by the Head and Fellows for varying periods according to the nature of the Fellowship. Their choice in neither case is confined to members of their own college or even to Oxford University. There have been and are Cambridge Heads of Oxford colleges and many colleges have men from Cambridge and other universities among their Fellows. Most Fellows are engaged in college teaching or administration. Since 1926 every holder of a professorial Chair in the University has been a Fellow of one or other of the colleges: thus the Regius Professor of Modern History is normally a Fellow of Oriel; the Harmsworth Professor of American History a Fellow of Queen's; the Heather Professor of Music a Fellow of Wadham. Most Fellows hold

[1] Answers to questions put by the Royal Commissioners of 1871 showed that the University possessed 7,683 acres and the colleges 184,764 acres. Christ Church had 30,000 acres and Magdalen 27,000. The total income of the University was £47,000 and of the colleges and halls £366,000; Christ Church had £57,000, Magdalen £39,000, New College £31,000. (Mallet, op. cit. iii. 334–5.)

University lecturerships or readerships which they combine with their college duties.

Besides its Head and Fellows every one of the old colleges except All Souls has undergraduates and all except All Souls, some graduate research students. Those 'on the foundation' as scholars, having been elected by special examination, receive certain emoluments and privileges. In particular they wear a more lengthy gown than the 'commoner' and in chapel they used always to wear surplices, as do the Head and Fellows, but this is not now always the case. It is the usual practice for undergraduates to spend at least their first two years in college and any later years in lodgings.

Since 1937 five colleges have been founded for postgraduate study, Nuffield, St. Antony's, Linacre, St. Cross, and Wolfson.

There are three terms during the year, each of eight weeks, Michaelmas, Hilary, Trinity.

The University, which consists virtually of the sum total of all the members of the colleges, is governed by its Chancellor (who since the close of the fifteenth century has generally been a non-resident nobleman or bishop); its Vice-Chancellor, the Vice-Chancellor-elect, the two Proctors, the Assessor, the Vice-Chairman of the General Board, and eighteen elected members of the Hebdomadal (i.e. weekly) Council. The Hebdomadal Council is a sort of 'cabinet' and the University's 'parliament' is Congregation which meets during term on Tuesdays in the Convocation House. It consists of all resident Doctors and Masters occupying official teaching or administrative positions in the University or colleges and numbers about 1,800. A larger body, called Convocation, consists of all M.A.s, Doctors of Divinity, Civil Law, and Medicine, and holders of certain other degrees: their number is estimated at over 35,000, mostly living away from Oxford, many, indeed, at the ends of the earth. A full meeting would be impossible, but Convocation still has certain functions such as the election of the Chancellor and the Professor of Poetry (a five-year appointment).

The Vice-Chancellor used to hold office for three years, but in 1957 the period was reduced to two; now, since 1969, it is four. Heads of colleges used to take the office in turn in order of seniority of election and subject to an age limit; but now any member of Congregation (subject also to an age limit) is eligible for election, and nomination is by a committee which proposes a name to Congregation for appointment as Vice-Chancellor. The Proctors hold office for a year and take office in March. Their duties are multifarious, for they serve on every important committee and are concerned also with University discipline. They come from different colleges which elect in pairs on a fixed twelve-year cycle. Thus Keble College is always linked with Corpus Christi and Merton College with Lincoln in the provision of Proctors. Proctors are always Fellows of their colleges and must be of a certain standing, neither too junior nor too senior. Since 1960 the five women's colleges and the five new post-graduate colleges in rotation elect one of their members, called the Assessor, to act with the Proctors. The principal permanent administrative officers of the University are the Registrar, the Secretary for Administration, the Secretary of the Chest, the Secretary of Faculties, and the Surveyor to the University.

Before the era of printing, and indeed for long after, books were scarce and precious and both teaching and examinations were conducted orally, largely by public disputation between *opponents* and *respondents*. Unfortunately the old system, though overhauled in the Laudian Statutes of 1632, fell into decay in the eighteenth century when the degree examinations became almost a farce.[1] The movement for reform, however, bore fruit in 1800 when a new Examination Statute was passed providing for Honours and Pass degrees. The principal subjects of study were still Classics and Mathematics and the first man to take a 'double First' was Sir Robert Peel in 1808. As the century advanced the field

[1] It is said that Lord Eldon, taking his B.A. degree in Hebrew and History was asked two questions: what is the Hebrew for the place of a skull, to which he replied 'Golgotha', and who founded University College, to which he replied 'Alfred the Great'.

II

of study was widened and faculties multiplied, so that there are now not only Faculties of Theology, Law, Medicine, and *Literae Humaniores* (the original Arts Faculty, commonly called 'Greats'), but also Faculties of Modern History, English, Modern Languages, Oriental Studies, Physical Sciences and Mathematics, Biological and Agricultural Sciences, Social Studies, Anthropology and Geography, Music, and Psychological Studies. Work and examinations are co-ordinated by Faculty Boards and by a General Board on which all the Faculties are represented.

Honours examinations in all Faculties are held in June each year and Class Lists are issued. To get a First in any 'School' or subject is a great distinction and colleges pride themselves on the numbers of Firsts which their members achieve. The written examinations consist of about twelve three-hour papers and are followed by a viva-voce examination. The usual course for a first degree, Bachelor of Arts, B.A., is three years, but in Classics, the 'Greats' School, it is four years. There is no further examination for the M.A. degree, which may be taken on payment of the necessary fees, seven years after matriculation. Many students taking high honours in Final Schools stay up for research and take higher degrees, e.g. B.D. (Bachelor of Divinity); B.C.L. (Bachelor of Civil Law); B.Litt. (Bachelor of Letters); B.Mus. (Bachelor of Music); B.Phil. (Bachelor of Philosophy); M.Sc. (Master of Science); or D.Phil. (Doctor of Philosophy), which may be taken in any subject. The first degrees in Medicine and Surgery are B.M. (Bachelor of Medicine), and B.Ch. (Bachelor of Chirurgerie). The degrees of D.D., D.C.L., D.M., D.Litt., D.Sc., and D.Mus. are reserved for the highest achievements in scholarship.

Jealous as the colleges are of their academic standing and reputation—and there are many University prizes to be competed for as well as Firsts in the Schools—the normal undergraduate indulges a lively concern for the fortunes of his college on the games field and on the river. Every college puts out representative teams in all the principal games, from rowing, cricket, rugby and association football, to bridge and chess, and the greatest honour is to be chosen to represent the University against Cambridge and thus to acquire a 'Blue' or, in the lesser games, a 'Half-Blue'. Every college has its own games field and so have the various University clubs. University cricket matches are played in the Parks. College rowing takes place on the Thames, mostly between Folly Bridge and Iffley Lock, but the University boat-race is rowed in London from Putney to Mortlake. The rugger and soccer matches against Cambridge and the Athletic Sports also take place in London.

In May 1964 the University agreed that its representatives on the City Council should be reduced from 12 to 8 (six councillors and two aldermen, instead of nine and three), and that they should be elected by Congregation instead of by Convocation and by Heads and bursars.

A CONDUCTED TOUR

UNTIL 1914 or even later most visitors would arrive by train and approach the city from the railway station, but now motor-cars, too many of them, come from all directions and may discharge their passengers anywhere. Thus the choice of a point from which to begin a tour of the city is bound to be arbitrary, especially as the colleges are closely grouped in an area more or less circular and are not strung out in a long line—with a few outliers—as at Cambridge. Moreover, despite its architectural magnificence in a score of aspects, many of Oxford's loveliest things must be sought out. New College is hidden down a narrow walled lane and its garden with the city walls around it is seen only by those who pass through the College. Wadham, St. John's, and Worcester gardens, even the Magdalen river walks and groves, are out of sight of the passer-by. Nor do the peace and quiet of Christ Church Meadow, with its shady Cherwell paths, thrust themselves upon the attention, as do the Backs at Cambridge. There is no through way in most of these places and they must be hunted out if their charm is to be enjoyed. Who could guess, for instance, from the simple and humble exterior of St. Edmund Hall, that it conceals such an enchanting quadrangle?

In general it may be said that every college and most of the University buildings and city churches are worth visiting, each having something unique as well as beautiful. University buildings may usually be visited at any time on week-days, but not always after 1 p.m. on Saturdays. Colleges are normally open every day after 1 p.m. until 5 or 7 in the summer, but close earlier in the winter (see full list, p. vii). Visitors severely pressed for time should try to see Christ Church, Magdalen, and New College at least, with eyes wide open for all that is between as they go from one to the other.

Starting at Carfax, or perhaps from the Information

Centre a few yards down St. Aldate's, we find ourselves in the middle of the ancient city where the highways have always crossed, running from east to west and south to north. The name is obscure, some deriving it from the Latin *quadrifurcus*, four-forked, and others from the French, *quatre voies*, four ways. At the north-west corner stands the fourteenth-century west tower of the former City Church of St. Martin. The body of the church formerly protruded into Cornmarket Street, making the roadway so narrow that, though it had been rebuilt as late as 1820, it was demolished in 1896, and the parish of St. Martin's was merged with that of All Saints' (see p. 94). Part of the old churchyard may be seen behind the Midland Bank. Under the east window of the church for several centuries was 'Pennyless Bench', the resort of beggars and loungers whose equally unspiritual but less colourful descendants still frequent the place, though bench and name are alike forgotten.

Another obstruction of former days was the Conduit erected in 1617 in the middle of Carfax at the cost of Otho Nicholson, also a benefactor of Christ Church. It usually flowed with water brought from Hinksey Hill, but on occasions of great rejoicing wine was substituted. It is a large and elaborate piece of Jacobean sculpture and was removed to Nuneham Park in 1787, as a present to Lord Harcourt.

Going southwards down St. Aldate's or 'St. Old's', formerly Fysshe Street, we pass the Town Hall on our left. It was built, in a florid pseudo-Jacobean style, in 1893–7 and replaced a dignified Georgian structure which was, no doubt, too small and inconvenient but did at least fit the scene. Underneath it is a fifteenth-century crypt, and behind the modern Town Hall in Norman and Plantagenet days was the wealthy Jewry with its synagogue.

On our right is Pembroke Street, occupied on the south side by the delightfully restored old houses which have been incorporated into the new quadrangle of Pembroke College. This leads to

ST. EBBE'S CHURCH in St. Ebbe's Street. There are remains of a twelfth-century door, carefully restored. The tower is thirteenth century with a modern top stage and the bulk of the church was rebuilt in 1814. There is some interesting heraldic glass and fine old communion plate, including a cup of 1569.

Beyond St. Ebbe's was Little Gate and hereabouts were the convents of the Franciscans (Paradise Square) and the Dominicans (by the river).

Returning to St. Aldate's, a little farther on, on the right we come to ST. ALDATE'S CHURCH, which probably owes its name to a forgotten pre-Norman saint. Nothing now visible is older than the fourteenth century, apart from a row of small Norman columns against the east wall of the north aisle. The south aisle, with crypt under, dates from *c.* 1320, and over it was a room, removed in 1862, long used as the library of Pembroke College, which also had the aisle as its chapel until its own was consecrated in 1732. The church was drastically restored in the nineteenth century, but contains interesting monuments, including the tomb of Robert Halle, a fifteenth-century Principal of Broadgates Hall, some very attractive brasses executed in memory of early seventeenth-century students who died at Broadgates Hall, and a fifteenth-century font. There are six bells dated 1620–54. For many years St. Aldate's has been the centre in Oxford of a lively evangelical churchmanship.

Enclosing the church on the south and west sides is:

PEMBROKE COLLEGE

Founded 1624. *Present strength*: The Master and 29 Fellows; 9 lecturers; 59 scholars, 30 exhibitioners; 276 B.A.s and commoners. *Buildings*: gatehouse, 1673–94 (Gothicized, 1830); chapel, 1732; hall, 1846; library (formerly hall), 1620; first quadrangle, 1626–70 (altered 1830–8); second quadrangle, 1844–8; Master's Lodgings, formerly Wolsey's almshouses, *c.* 1524; north quadrangle, 16th–20th centuries.

IN 1624 Broadgates Hall, one of the more prosperous medieval halls and mainly used by law students, became Pembroke College. It was nominally founded by King James I and took its name from William, third Earl of Pembroke, who was then Chancellor of the University, but its endowments came from

16

Thomas Tesdale and Richard Wightwick, who were specially interested in providing scholarships and Fellowships for their own kin and for boys from Abingdon School, with which the College still preserves a close connexion. The last Principal of Broadgates Hall was the first Master of Pembroke. King Charles I in 1636 and Bishop Morley of Winchester in 1678 founded scholarships for boys from the Channel Islands and, since the College was never wealthy, Queen Anne provided an adequate stipend for the Master by attaching to his office a canonry of Gloucester Cathedral. This was, however, disannexed in 1938. The late Lord Nuffield was a munificent benefactor.

The College occupies the site of half a dozen medieval halls, the chief of which were Broadgates Hall and Beef Hall, and the refectory of Broadgates is now the College library, a new and rather fine hall having been built in 1848. The southern boundary of the College is the old city wall. The Master's Lodgings, formerly Wolsey's alms houses, face St. Aldate's and are a charming example of sixteenth-century domestic architecture, but the front of the College is disappointing. Formerly, at the end of a simple seventeenth-century range there came a low gatehouse tower of three stages, hardly surmounting the neighbouring roofs, with classical balustrading and other Renaissance details. An Oxford builder, Daniel Evans, was employed to modify all this, adding a fourth stage to the tower, eliminating the dormers from the old roof-line, substituting a full third story with battlements, and thus transforming the whole into a false Gothic (1830-8). It is all rather insignificant—not a bold and dramatic villainy as was perpetrated by Waterhouse at Balliol, but more like a sneaking peccadillo up a side-street. In summer the quadrangle is gay with window boxes and virginia creeper, the most colourful in Oxford.

The chapel is a pleasant piece of early-eighteenth-century work with original stalls and screen. The altar-piece is a copy by Cranke after Rubens's painting of the Risen Christ and the ceiling and windows are by Kempe, 1884.

The latest addition to the College, the Besse Building, is in what was Beef Lane. This little-used street was closed in

1960 and the old houses to the north were adapted to make one side of a new and picturesque quadrangle.

Famous men: Edmund Bonner, Bishop of London; Francis Beaumont, the playwright; William Camden, the antiquary; Sir Thomas Browne, author of *Religio Medici*; John Pym, the great parliamentarian; George Whitefield, the Methodist; Samuel Johnson (whose portrait by Reynolds and whose tea-pot are in the Senior Common Room); Sir William Blackstone, the author of *Commentaries on the Laws of England* (1765-9); and J. W. Fulbright.

Coming out of Pembroke and returning to St. Aldate's we get an impressive view of Tom Tower of Christ Church, but turning to the right we continue past Pembroke to Brewer Street, which runs westward under the old city wall. In it we shall find the Christ Church Cathedral School where the boys of the choir and others are prepared for admission to Public Schools at the age of 13½, and just beyond it is

CAMPION HALL

Founded 1896. *Present strength*: The Master; a Bursar; a Treasurer; 10 tutors; 40 commoners.

 IN 1918 a Statute was passed empowering the Vice-Chancellor, subject to the consent of Convocation, to grant licences for the establishment of Permanent Private Halls so long as they were formally constituted on a non-profit-making basis. Convocation's approval is also required for the appointment of Masters or Principals who must be Masters of Arts of the University. Students admitted must be presented for matriculation in the same way as other undergraduates and are subject to the same University regulations.

It was in accordance with this Statute that a Private Hall for members of the Society of Jesus, hitherto known successively as Clarke's Hall, Pope's Hall, and Plater's Hall, was set up as Campion Hall, taking its name from Edmund Campion, Fellow of St. John's, who was martyred for his faith in 1581. Until 1935 it was in St. Giles'.

The present buildings, designed by Sir Edwin Lutyens,

18

O.M., incorporate parts of an ancient house, Micklem Hall, and though the site is restricted they are a strikingly original addition to the Oxford scene, the chapel and library being particularly good.

Returning to St. Aldate's and continuing southward to Folly Bridge, we pass on the right the admirably restored Old Palace built by Thomas Smith *c.* 1622 and incorporating on the west an older house. It is a picturesque gabled mansion with carved mullioned and transomed windows and pargeted plasterwork. There are fine seventeenth-century panelling and plaster ceilings within. The house is now the headquarters of the Roman Catholic chaplaincy to the University.

A little farther on we pass the old Littlemore Hall, now two houses numbered 82 and 83. Recently restored, they are a good example of fifteenth-century work largely rebuilt in the seventeenth century, with fine plaster ceilings, friezes, and panelling. No. 83 is supposed to have been the shop kept by the Sheep with the knitting-needles in Lewis Carroll's *Through the Looking Glass.*

St. Aldate's crosses the River Thames or Isis[1] by way of an island at Folly Bridge, the probable site of the original *Oxenford.*[2] There was a bridge here in 1220 and until 1779 half-way across it stood a tower and gateway, probably part of the defences of the city, but traditionally a point of vantage from which Roger Bacon (*c.* 1214–94) studied astronomy. This tower seems to have been known successively as Bachelor's Tower, Friar Bacon's study, and the Folly.

From the bridge, looking east, the line of college barges strung out along the left bank of the river, and backed by the elms of Christ Church Meadow, used to make a splendid sight, especially during Eights Week when the flags flew from the poles and every barge-roof bore its burden of pretty

[1] The name *Isis* was used for the River Thames above its junction with the River Thame at Dorchester. The Latin name for the Thames was *Tamesis* and to the ignorant this looked like Thame + Isis, hence the two names for the same river.

[2] The late H. E. Salter says, however, that the original Ox-ford was at Hinksey Ferry: see his Ford Lectures, *Medieval Oxford* (Oxf. Hist. Soc. 1936), pp. 1–3.

dresses and brilliant blazers. But, alas, the scene has changed and the barges have given place to boat-houses that look like boot-boxes, which, adding insult to injury, have also displaced the trees.

A walk along the towpath past the Oxford University Boat House to Iffley brings one to where the Eights and Torpids races begin and to Iffley Church, still one of the most perfectly preserved twelfth-century parish churches in England. The only extension since it was built has been the addition of one bay to the chancel *c*. 1250.

From Folly Bridge we turn back up St. Aldate's. Salter's boat-building yard, to the right, is an attractive group of eighteenth-century buildings. A little farther on are the drab and unprepossessing Headquarters of the City Police, a monument to the skinflint economies of the early nineteen-thirties, and next, behind a green lawn, are the buildings of

LINACRE COLLEGE

Founded 1962. *Present strength*: The Principal; 37 Fellows; 6 Junior Research Fellows; 199 members receiving tuition or supervision.

LINACRE College began in 1962 as a Society for men and women graduates, mostly from other universities, whether British or foreign, who want to read for advanced degrees or diplomas in any subject. Its students do not live in the College, but usually in lodgings. It has ranked as a self-governing college of the University since 1965.

It takes its name from the great Renaissance scholar and physician, Thomas Linacre, Fellow of All Souls in 1484, friend of Colet, More, and Erasmus and founder of the College of Physicians in London. And its buildings, designed by Sir Hubert Worthington, were those of St. Catherine's Society from 1936 till 1962, in which year St. Catherine's moved to Holywell Great Meadow and became a college (see p. 144).

1. Pembroke College: front quadrangle

2. The Isis in Eights Week

3. Christ Church: Tom Tower from Tom Quad

CHRIST CHURCH

Founded (by Wolsey) 1525; *refounded* (by Henry VIII) 1532 and again in 1546. *Present strength*: The Dean; 5 Canons (four of whom are Professors in the Faculty of Theology); 47 Students (known as Fellows in other colleges); 23 lecturers; 102 scholars, 67 exhibitioners; 2 chaplains; organist; 6 singing men; 8 choristers; 279 other members receiving tuition or supervision. *Buildings*: gatehouse, 1525/1681; Cathedral, twelfth- to nineteenth-century; Chapter House, thirteenth-century, but with twelfth-century doorway; former dormitory, thirteenth-century; former refectory, fifteenth-century; cloister, *c.* 1500–5; hall and kitchen, 1529; vaulted roof of hall staircase, 1640; south, east, and west sides of Great Quadrangle (Tom Quad), 1529; north side, *c.* 1640–63; Peckwater quadrangle, 1706–11; library, 1761; Anatomy school, now museum, 1766; Canterbury quadrangle, 1773–8; Meadow Buildings, 1862–5; hall staircase tower, 1876–9; Picture Gallery, 1968; Blue Boar range, 1969.

'MAJESTIC' is the adjective likeliest to spring to mind as one approaches Christ Church, often called 'the House' from its Latin title *Aedes Christi*, or House of Christ. There is not only Wren's sugar-castor tower, standing in the midst of a noble balustraded front, but to the right, lifting itself as on a cliff over the grey walls of the colourful Memorial Garden (1926), is the long line of pinnacles, eleven of them, crowning the buttresses which separate the windows of the great hall and at the east end of this is the squat tower with four turrets which covers the vaulted staircase and contains the twelve 'merry Christ Church bells'. If one is coming the other way, along Cornmarket Street, from the north, Tom Tower is the jewel in the centre of the picture and seems to dominate the scene.

But we are coming from the south. We pass the fine wrought-iron gates (by R. M. Y. Gleadowe) which give entrance to the Memorial Garden (laid out by John Coleridge to commemorate Christ Church men who gave their lives in the First World War) and Christ Church Meadow and go straight up to the main gate with its original massive oak doors. Loggan's view, 1675, shows the front as it is now, with the great double-turreted wings and bay windows at either end and the elaborate Tudor turrets on either side of the main gate, but the Gothic ogee windows and octagonal tower with its ogee cupola above, are missing. These were designed and added by Wren in 1681, an original and unique contribution to the Oxford sky-line.

Wolsey planned things on a scale never before attempted, but both the constitution and the fabric of his College bear the marks of his fall. His statue over the great gate dates from 1719, a belated tribute erected by Jonathan Trelawney, one of his successors in the See of Winchester. The cloisters of the spacious quadrangle, the largest in Oxford, and a little smaller than the Great Court at Trinity, Cambridge, were never built, though the plinths are there and the arcading (renewed in the nineteenth century) in the wall from which the arches would have sprung. The great hall he finished and the kitchen, but the chapel he proposed all along the north side of the quadrangle never got beyond the foundations, and it was only in the seventeenth century (c. 1640–63) that the site was filled with lodgings for clergy.

It is said that Wolsey intended to sweep away the monastic church altogether. He pulled down the three west bays of the nave to make room for his quadrangle, the result being that Christ Church is one of the smallest cathedrals in England. He also destroyed the Church of St. Michael-at-the-South-Gate and a stretch of the city wall, and he incorporated the buildings of Peckwater Inn and Canterbury College. Elsewhere Wolsey had, with royal and papal permission, suppressed twenty monastic houses to provide the money for his twin foundations of the school at Ipswich and the College at Oxford. Ipswich School was hardly started and came to nothing, but Henry VIII took over and completed what Wolsey had begun in Oxford, enriching the College with substantial endowments. Although under the King there were to be only eight Canons instead of sixty, the student body was increased to compensate for this reduction. The cathedral of the new See of Oxford was also moved from Oseney Abbey, where it had been established in 1542, to Christ Church, which thus became a unique combination of College and Cathedral Chapter, the Dean presiding over both: Oseney Abbey has now all but disappeared.

As we stand in the gateway and look up, we see forty-eight coats of arms, which include those of many royal and noble benefactors, such as Wolsey, Henry VIII, Charles II, and James, Duke of York. Above, in the bell chamber is the great bell called 'Great Tom', cast in 1680 by Christopher Hodson to replace the original bell of that name which came from Oseney Abbey. It weighs over six tons and rings 101 times every night at 9.5 p.m. (9 p.m. by the Oxford meridian). Until early in this century this was the curfew when all college gates were shut and men coming in later paid gate-money. The number, 101, was the number of members 'on the foundation'.

On the east side of the tower is a statue of Queen Anne. The fountain dates from 1670, but the figure of Mercury was replaced for the third time as recently as 1928.

In the south-east corner of the quadrangle are the entrances to the hall and the Cathedral, but as they make no break in the general design they might go almost unnoticed.

The hall is reached by a grand staircase built by Wyatt in 1805 beneath the remarkably late fan-vaulting of one Smith, artificer of London, employed by Dean Samuel Fell in 1640. It is the largest medieval hall in Oxford, $114\frac{1}{2}$ ft. × $39\frac{3}{4}$ ft., and compares with that at Trinity, Cambridge, built in 1604, which is 100 ft. × 40 ft. The roof is of the hammer-beam type, richly carved and gilded. The panelling is early nineteenth-century and from it hangs the finest collection of portraits in any of the Oxford colleges. Painters represented include Lely, Kneller, Reynolds, Gainsborough, Romney, and Lawrence, and for many years now every picture added has meant the exclusion of an older one. Among the more notable subjects are John Locke, John Wesley, George Grenville (of Stamp Act fame), George Canning, W. E. Gladstone. It is odd that the only figure in armour is the Quaker, William Penn. Lovers of *Alice in Wonderland* will notice the picture of C. L. Dodgson, the real name of Lewis Carroll. There are many Prime Ministers, Governors-General and Viceroys of India, judges, bishops, and philosophers, but, curiously enough, poets are scarcely represented.

On the right, leaving the hall, are the steps down to the kitchen, a vast chamber open to the timbered roof. The old chopping-block is there, the great elm table replaced in 1949 after 210 years' service, and the old grids which held the glowing charcoal against the wall and in front of which the turnspits turned the joints: the smoke travelled up the wall and out through the open louvre in the middle of the roof.

A way leads from the kitchen back to the foot of the great stairs and out into the fifteenth-century cloister, the western third of which was cut off by Wolsey. Behind and above it, to the right, is the former *frater* or refectory of the Canons of St. Frideswide, now divided into undergraduate sets of rooms. Over the right-hand corner and at the east end of the *frater* is the former *dorter* (dormitory) and opposite, in the middle of the east side of the cloister is the fine thirteenth-century Chapter House with its twelfth-century doorway. To the left is the Cathedral, the ancient monastic church. The round-headed windows proclaim that they date from the twelfth century and the sharp-pointed lancets of the upper stage of the tower and of the spire, from the thirteenth. The spire is probably the oldest in England, massive but not graceful.

A door in the north-west corner of the cloister leads into the Cathedral. Looking along the narrow nave from the organ screen to the High Altar one gets a misleading impression of length and it is not at all apparent that the shape of the building is more nearly square than the usual oblong. Two features at once strike the eye, the massive twelfth-century Norman pillars and the exquisite fifteenth-century vaulting of the choir. Next one may notice the unusual feature of double arches: the main arches rising from the capitals sustain an upper triforium while lower arches between the pillars uphold a lower triforium. It is an unusual and skilful device for giving an impression of height. But possibly the main factor giving the illusion of length is Scott's brilliant east end which arrests the attention immediately one enters the building. The stalls of the nave and choir are Victorian and during term are reserved for members of the House, all of whom wear surplices at the College services on Sundays. The pulpit is a fine piece of Jacobean work and Charles I must have listened to many sermons preached from it during the Civil War when Oxford was his headquarters and the Deanery his residence.

Turning to the left into the north aisle we see the west window, by Abraham van Linge, showing Jonah and Nineveh. This artist is also represented by windows in the north transept and, fragmentarily, in the east window of St. Lucy's Chapel, which also has fourteenth-century glass in its tracery.

The north transept is a good place for hearing both sermon and choir. To the east of it are the Latin Chapel (*c.* 1320), the Lady Chapel (mid thirteenth century) and the north choir aisle. The first is distinguished by its dark oak sixteenth-century stalls, the fine seventeenth-century Vice-Chancellor's throne and the fourteenth-century glass of the north windows. Between it and the Lady Chapel are some interesting tombs. First is one with an effigy formerly thought to be of Sir George Nowers, early fifteenth century, though the tomb and effigy do not belong to each other. Next to this is an altar tomb, with an effigy ascribed to Prior Sutton (1316) under an early English canopy. Then there is the tomb of Elizabeth Montacute, 1354, who married first the second Lord Montague and then Thomas, Lord Furnival, and who gave the southern part of Christ Church Meadow to the Canons; and under the easternmost arch is a monument in stone with a watching chamber in oak above it, both finely carved (late fifteenth century). Opposite it and between the Lady Chapel and north choir aisle is the upper part of the shrine of St. Frideswide. It stands on a reconstructed base and probably dates from the second translation of her remains in 1289; the first translation was in 1181, but why they were moved nobody knows. The translations may have been connected with successive stages of the building. The spandrels of the canopy of the shrine contain notable examples of naturalistically carved foliage.

Above the so-called Nowers's tomb, affixed to a pillar, is a wall monument, with bust, of Robert Burton, 1639, author of *The Anatomy of Melancholy*. On the next pillar, between the Lady Chapel and the north choir aisle is the monument of William Goodwin, Dean 1611–20.

We may now cross under the central tower to the south transept, the southernmost bay of which we do not see because it was a passage from the cloister to the former cemetery and is now used as a sacristy.

Both in the south choir aisle and St. Lucy's Chapel (extended early in the fourteenth century) are many monuments to cavaliers and others who died during the Civil War, 1642–6. Under the arch between aisle and chapel is the tomb of Robert King, 1557, the last Abbot of Oseney and first Bishop of Oxford. He also appears in a window, probably by Bernard van Linge, in the south aisle. Here also is the regimental chapel of the Oxfordshire and Buckinghamshire Light Infantry, the 53rd Foot. There are many memorials of Deans and Canons. John Fell's is on the south wall of the antechapel and Henry Aldrich, who is buried under a slab in the Lady Chapel, has his effigy on the pillar next to the pulpit.

The organ was originally built by Bernhard Schmidt in 1680, but it has been rebuilt and enlarged. The case is of the same date. The Cathedral plate, which is displayed on the High Altar on the great festivals, includes a fine set of two chalices, two flagons, an alms dish, and two candlesticks, all dated 1660–1.

In the vestibule outside the west door is a memorial to those Christ Church men who fell in the two world wars.

Turning to the right we pass the door of the Deanery and go under Kill Canon tower with its statues of Dean Fell and Dean Liddell, into Peckwater quadrangle. This quadrangle, built 1705–13 to designs which are attributed to Dean Aldrich, occupies the site of Peckwater Inn which Wolsey suppressed. The soft Headington stone of which it was built became so weathered that the whole was refaced in 1931 and it now stands as one of the most gracious examples of Palladian architecture in Oxford. The practice of grassing more and more Oxford quadrangles grew up after the First World War: before that many were gravelled and 'Peck' was one of them. Others were those of St. John's, Lincoln, Oriel, and Exeter. Merton and Corpus still have gravel quadrangles, but they are the only survivors.

The library, refaced 1962–3, which bounds the south side

Christi Church
Cathedral choir

Blackwater quadrangle

5. Oriel College: first quadrangle

6. Corpus Christi College: front quadrangle and gate-tower

of Peckwater quadrangle and stands between it and the Dean's garden was begun in 1716 and built to the designs of another amateur architect, Dr. George Clarke, Fellow of All Souls, who also designed the front of Worcester. It is a magnificent but heavy building, lacking the grace of Aldrich's reputed work, but it had been Clarke's intention that the ground floor space should be an open loggia as is the case with Wren's library at Trinity College, Cambridge. This scheme, however, was frustrated by a succession of great legacies of books and pictures and the space that was meant to be airy and open was enclosed to house them. The delicate circular staircase leads to a magnificently furnished room which runs the whole length of the building. The bookcases line the walls and the floor is as free of obstructions as a tennis court. The iron work of the staircase, the plaster work of the ceilings, and the wood-work of the shelves and furniture are all splendid examples of eighteenth-century craftsmanship. Cardinal Wolsey's hat is in the display cabinet in which Horace Walpole kept it at Strawberry Hill.

From Peckwater quadrangle we go into the smaller Canterbury quadrangle, built 1773–83 by James Wyatt at the cost of Richard Robinson, Archbishop of Armagh. He desired that these spacious sets of rooms should be reserved always for noblemen and gentlemen commoners. This quadrangle stands on the site of Canterbury College, which was founded in 1361 and was originally intended to comprise monks from Christ Church, Canterbury, and secular scholars; of this John Wyclif was Warden, 1365–72. It was suppressed by Wolsey. It is in the SW. corner of this quadrangle that we may descend to the new picture gallery built at the cost of Sir Charles Forte to the designs of Messrs. Powell and Moya and opened by the Queen in 1968. The 300 paintings and 1,700 drawings, mainly the bequest of General John Guise in 1765, but with later additions, form the finest collection of Italian 'primitives' and other sixteenth- and seventeenth-century works possessed by any college.

Before we leave Christ Church by Wyatt's Doric gate, it should be mentioned that the House has another block of buildings erected in 1862–5 at the top of the Meadow. They are in Venetian Gothic and were inspired by Ruskin. The most recent range of buildings along Blue Boar Street is by Powell and Moya and incorporates the old brewery. To the south of the hall is 'Dr. Lee's Anatomy School', 1766, now used for the purposes of the Senior Common Room.

Famous men: these include thirteen Prime Ministers and eleven Governors-General of India, among them Canning, Peel, Gladstone, Salisbury, Wellesley, Dalhousie, Minto, and the late Lord Halifax. Others are Richard Hakluyt, Sir Philip Sidney, John Locke, William Penn, John Wesley, the seventh Earl of Shaftesbury, E. B. Pusey, C. L. Dodgson (Lewis Carroll), and W. H. Auden.

With Canterbury quadrangle behind us, we look along Merton Street. To our right is Corpus Christi College and to our left is

ORIEL COLLEGE

Founded 1326. *Present strength*: The Provost; 25 Fellows; 13 lecturers; 47 scholars; 36 exhibitioners, 239 other members receiving tuition or supervision. *Buildings*: gatehouse, 1620; chapel, hall, and first quadrangle, 1620–42; library, 1788; second quadrangle, 1720; third quadrangle, formerly St. Mary Hall, hall, and chapel, 1640; south-west corner *c.* 1450; Rhodes building, 1909–11.

A N oriel window is an upper-floor bay window protruding from the wall on a stone bracket or corbel and this College may have taken the nickname by which it is known from a feature in one of its original properties. The full-dress name of the College is 'the House of the Blessed Mary the Virgin in Oxford, commonly called Oriel College, of the Foundation of Edward II of famous memory, sometime King of England' and its arms are the King's three lions 'within a bordure engrailed argent'. But the real founder was Adam de Brome, the King's Almoner, Rector of St. Mary the Virgin, and he had the endowments of the church transferred to his College which, in consequence, has ever after appointed its vicars. Edward III gave the College the Hospital of St. Bartholomew

28

at Cowley, a convenient refuge in time of plague as well as a source of revenue.

Merton, in its Fellows' quadrangle, 1608, and Wadham, 1612, set a new fashion in collegiate architecture and Oriel and University Colleges decided to follow it. They demolished their medieval buildings and replaced them with picturesque examples of seventeenth-century Gothic. They may be contrasted with the slightly later work in Renaissance style at Clare and Christ's Colleges, Cambridge, work which has no counterpart in Oxford.

On entering Oriel we are faced by a line of late Gothic windows of hall and ante-chapel, surmounted by curvilinear Jacobean gables which are continued all round the quadrangle both internally and outside. Peeping over them is the pinnacled top of Merton Chapel tower. Opposite are a central porch and a flight of steps leading up to the hall. Above them are canopied statues of Edward II and Charles I and over them is a Virgin and Child surmounted by a classical cartouche and pediment.

The hall has a good hammer-beam roof and a Jacobean screen. The chapel has stalls, panelling, and screen of the seventeenth century in a restrained classical style, but the communion rails are richly carved. The lectern was given in 1654.

The second quadrangle is enclosed on the north side by Wyatt's rather ponderous library which contrasts pleasantly with the flanking Gothic. Below the library is the Senior Common Room.

Beyond these is the quadrangle of the former St. Mary Hall, for long dependent upon Oriel and finally incorporated in it in 1902. Its hall, with chapel above it, now Junior Common Room and junior library respectively, are immediately to the right, in the south-east corner, and opposite is the block built by Basil Champneys with part of the munificent bequest of Cecil Rhodes, the South African pioneer who gave his name to Rhodesia and endowed the Rhodes scholarships which bring to Oxford every year over thirty young men from Commonwealth countries, thirty-two from the United States, and two from West Germany. They now get

£900 a year each plus fees and since 1903 there have been nearly 4,000 of them.

The most famous time in Oriel's history began under the rule of Provost Eveleigh, 1781–1814, and was continued under his successors Edward Copleston, 1814–28, and Edward Hawkins, 1828–74. In these days the Oriel Common Room recruited John Keble; Richard Whateley, Archbishop of Dublin; Thomas Arnold, Headmaster of Rugby; J. H. Newman, Cardinal; E. B. Pusey; R. H. Froude; and R. W. Church, Dean of St. Paul's.

Other famous men: Thomas Arundel, Archbishop of Canterbury, 1396–1414, Cardinal William Allen, 1532–94, Sir Walter Ralegh, William Prynne, Gilbert White, Samuel Wilberforce, Tom Hughes (author of *Tom Brown's School Days*), and Cecil Rhodes.

If, on coming out of Oriel, we turn to the left and enter Merton Street we shall find immediately on our right the plain but dignified exterior of

CORPUS CHRISTI COLLEGE

Founded 1517. *Present strength*: The President; 25 Fellows; 5 research Fellows; 13 lecturers; 57 scholars; 29 exhibitioners; 160 B.A.s and commoners. *Buildings*: gatehouse, chapel, hall, library, first quadrangle, begun *c.* 1512; Fellows Building, 1706–12; President's Lodging, partly *c.* 1689, mostly 1904–6, with some reconstruction, 1958–60; Magpie Lane buildings, 1884 and 1969.

'CORPUS' has always been a small college, but it has never lacked quality and distinction. Its founder, Richard Fox, was a statesman-cleric typical of his day, successively Bishop of Exeter, Bath and Wells, Durham, and Winchester, Secretary (1485–7) and Lord Privy Seal (1487–1516) to Henry VII and Henry VIII, Chancellor of Cambridge and Master of Pembroke College there, 1507–18. Probably a Magdalen man, he was a benefactor of both universities, but it was at Oxford that he decided to found his College. His first intention was to found a house for the monks of St. Swithin's, Winchester, on the lines of the existing Benedictine colleges at Oxford—Durham, Gloucester Hall, and Canterbury College—but the future of monasteries being insecure, he was dissuaded from this by his friend, Hugh Oldham, Bishop of Exeter and founder of Manchester Grammar School. The result was a college for the training of secular clergy with special provision made in the statutes for the teaching of Latin, Greek, and Theology. Oldham contributed £4,000 to the costs.

A somewhat constricted site was bought between Merton and the street then running on the east side of Canterbury College, the southern boundary being the city wall. Yet small as the area was it had hitherto provided accommodation for six halls and their gardens, Urban Hall, St. Christopher's, Corner Hall, Nun Hall or Ledynporch, Nevil(e)'s Inn, Bekes Inn.

Provision was made for twenty Fellows and twenty *discipuli*, who were to be aged between twelve and seventeen at their admission. Each Fellow was responsible for one 'disciple' who shared rooms with him, the Fellow sleeping on a high bed and the pupil on a truckle bed. There was also room for four or at most six sons of noblemen or lawyers who might live in College at their own costs. The first President, John Claimond, a Magdalen man, was able, scholarly, and generous. He was an old friend of Fox and he died at the age of eighty, having ruled for twenty years. He bequeathed the sapphire ring left him by Fox to his successors, and his books to the College library.

The gate-tower contains a richly panelled room with an oriel window and a fine Tudor plaster ceiling. This room, together with various others on either side of the gate, was the quarters of the Head of the College, and from there the President could keep an eye upon all that went on within and without. The hall, in the east range, is small but has a good original hammer-beam roof and early-eighteenth-century panelling. Until a fire-place was inserted in 1741 it was heated by a charcoal brazier. The library extends along much of the first floor of the south range; though the building and some of the plasterwork dates from the early sixteenth century, the fittings and the plasterwork are for the most part early seventeenth century. It is extremely picturesque and still retains the apparatus for chaining books, though the chains are gone. There is a valuable collection of manuscripts.

The chapel, reached through a passage in the south-east corner of the quadrangle, is in line with the library. There is a beautiful classical screen of cedar wood carrying the arms of the House of Stuart. It and the stalls date from 1675. The altar-piece, *The Adoration of the Shepherds* (given by Sir Richard Worsley, Bt., in 1804) is most probably a seventeenth-century copy after Rubens.

Beyond the chapel are the Cloister quadrangle and the handsome Fellows' Building erected by President Turner in 1706–12 and possibly designed by Dean Aldrich. The front on to the garden is particularly gracious: it was refaced in 1956. The Gentlemen-Commoners' Building between the Senior Common Room and the kitchen was completely rebuilt in 1737 and at the corner of the footpath into the Meadow is the Thomas Building, 1928, named after Emily Thomas, who gave the College £100,000 in 1919. On the other side of the street, at the bottom of Magpie Lane, is an annexe, built by Sir T. G. Jackson, R.A., in 1884–5, one of his least successful works, and just beyond it another range has replaced some early nineteenth-century houses (Powell and Moya).

The Presidents had a house of their own from 1607 in the south-west corner of the College, although the present building dates mostly from 1904–6. It was remodelled and reduced in size in 1958–60, when some undergraduate rooms were added.

The sundial in the middle of the gravelled quadrangle surmounted with a pelican was put up in 1581 and the perpetual calendar was added to its pillar in 1606.

By some means Corpus contrived to retain its gold and silver plate, secular as well as ecclesiastical when all the other colleges surrendered their secular plate to Charles I in 1642. It thus has some priceless treasures including the brilliant late-fifteenth-century silver-gilt bishop's staff of the Founder and a superb silver-gilt standing salt and cover, as well as the Founder's gold communion vessels (1507).

Famous men: Richard Hooker, author of *The Treatise on the Laws of Ecclesiastical Polity*; John Jewel, Bishop of Salisbury, to whom the Church of England owed so much in the difficult days of Queen Elizabeth I; John Rainolds, President 1598–1607, one of the translators of the Authorized Version of the Bible; Nicholas Udall; General Oglethorpe (founder of Georgia); William Scott, Lord Stowell; John Keble and Thomas Arnold, both of whom became Fellows of Oriel; Sir Henry Newbolt, Robert Bridges, poets.

Next to Corpus Christi and along the cobbled Merton Street, known throughout the Middle Ages as St. John's Street, stands

MERTON COLLEGE

Founded 1264. *Present strength*: The Warden; 41 Fellows; 7 Visiting Research Fellows; 15 lecturers; 46 postmasters; 35 exhibitioners; 5 Harmsworth and 2 Domus Senior Scholars; 236 other members receiving tuition or supervision. *Buildings*: gatehouse, 1418; chapel: choir, 1290–4, transepts, 1367–8, 1424; bell-tower, 1450; hall before 1277 (much restored); library, 1373–8; Mob Quad, 1304–11; Fellows' quadrangle, 1608–10; Fitzjames gateway, 1497; gateway west of hall, 1510; sacristy, 1309; Grove Buildings, 1864, reconstructed 1930; St. Alban quadrangle, 1905–10; Rose Lane buildings, 1939–40; Warden's Lodging, 1963.

 COMPARED with the neat quadrangles we have already seen, Merton College seems to be an undisciplined group of buildings, but that is not surprising in the pioneer college, for to Merton must be accorded the honour of primacy despite the claims of University and Balliol Colleges, which enjoyed precedence in the *University Calendar* until 1970, when alphabetical order prevailed.

In 1262 Walter de Merton 'sometime Chancellor of the illustrious lord, Henry, King of England', later Bishop of Rochester, allotted the revenues of his manors of Maldon and Farleigh in Surrey for the support of 'clerks' studying at a university and next year he established eight of his nephews, sons of five of his sisters, at Oxford in one of the halls and also made provision for the inclusion of others not of his kin. For this he got the approval of Henry III and of

33

the Bishop and Chapter of Winchester. In 1264 he obtained their sanction to a new scheme establishing twenty scholars at Oxford, or some other university. The deed of this, most beautifully written, and with the seals complete, is still in the Merton archives. In 1270 the plan was further enlarged and in August 1274 a final set of statutes was drawn up whereby the College was definitely established in Oxford.

The first plot of land was bought in January 1266 and with it came the advowson of the Church of St. John Baptist which stood a little to the south of the present chapel. Adjoining properties were gradually added so that the greater part of the land and houses were acquired between the city wall on the east and St. Frideswide's on the west, and between the wall to the south and the street. The Founder also secured for his College the advowsons of the churches of St. Peter-in-the-East and St. Cross, with the valuable royal manor of Holywell just outside the city wall. It may well be that something survives of one of the original properties, Flixthorpe's house, in the building somewhat to the east of the present gate-tower. It was there that the first Warden, Peter of Abingdon, took up his residence in 1274. He bought houses and land on the other side of the street where Postmasters' Hall now stands.

'The foundation of Merton', writes the late Dr. H. W. Garrod, 'is memorable as the first great permanent endowment of learning in England',[1] but what the founder had mainly in mind was, first, the advantage of his own kin and, secondly, the provision of men well qualified to serve in Church and State; a Fellow had to give up his Fellowship if he left the College or obtained a benefice or entered a religious order.

In the earliest years many of the *scholares, parvuli, pueri,* were very young and had to be prepared for admission to the University and some of them continued to live in the town, in *hospitia* or halls until 1349. Others were undergraduates reading for the B.A. degree and the rest were Fellows, living in relative comfort in College. In 1280 there were about forty Fellows in College and twenty-five under-

[1] *V.C.H. Oxfordshire,* iii. 104.

graduates living out. Dr. Garrod[1] points out that this number was larger than Balliol, Exeter, Oriel, University, and Queen's Colleges together could muster seventy years later. Only a very small proportion of the total student population yet lived in colleges, perhaps one-fifteenth altogether.

In 1380 John Wylliott, a former Fellow, endowed a number of scholarships which were tenable for five years and those who held them, together with the other scholars, came to be known as *portionistae*, later corrupted into *postmasters*, by which name scholars of Merton are still called.

For many years the College specialized in the production of mathematicians and natural philosophers or scientists. At the time of the Renaissance, however, Warden Fitzjames, otherwise a benefactor, set himself against the New Learning and, as Bishop of London, persecuted Colet, the great Dean of St. Paul's.

In the seventeenth century Merton was Puritan in sympathy, though during the Civil War the Warden's Lodgings were occupied by Queen Henrietta Maria while Charles I lived in the Deanery at Christ Church. Anthony à Wood, however, the gossip and diarist to whom Oxford history owes so much, was a stout cavalier. His monument is in the ante-chapel, as also are monuments to Sir Thomas Bodley, a Magdalen man who became a Fellow of Merton, and Sir Henry Savile (Brasenose), who combined the offices of Warden of Merton, 1585–1622, and Provost of Eton, 1596–1622. He founded the Savilian Professorships of Geometry and Astronomy, both now attached to New College.

The old buildings of Merton are not only attractive in themselves but are also interesting as being in several instances the first of their kind.

The gate-tower dates from 1418 when Henry V gave permission for its crenellation. The statues which represent the Founder and, presumably, King Henry III are reproductions of older ones, but the panel with the *Agnus Dei* and John Baptist and various animals belongs to the fifteenth century. The doors are original. The wing to the west is seventeenth century but that to the east incorporates part

[1] *V.C.H. Oxfordshire*, iii. 104.

35

of the original Warden's Lodging, which is late thirteenth century.

Unfortunately the hall is not what it was. We know it was glazed in 1291, but it was so severely reconstructed by James Wyatt in 1794 and restored by Gilbert Scott in 1874, that only the walls at either end and the extraordinary door with its wrought-iron work are probably original.

To the west is a passage which passes the ancient sacristy and treasury, the oldest collegiate buildings in Oxford, and takes us into Mob Quad. It is Oxford's oldest quadrangle, but no one can account for its name. The east and north sides were built first and the library is on the south and west sides: the oldest part of this, which is on the first floor, was built at the cost of Bishop Rede of Chichester, 1371–9. It is the oldest library in England, but even so it had a predecessor which had to be repaired in 1338 and again in 1346–9. It is a lovely ∟-shaped room with shelves and furnishings of the late sixteenth and early seventeenth centuries. A few books are still chained as an example of their former state. The shelves and reading-desks, all in oak, are at right angles to the walls and narrow windows let the light into the bays. Dormer windows were inserted in the roof in the next century. The sixteenth-century German glass in the east window was inserted in c. 1840, and the glass in the east windows of the west wing is fifteenth-century. There is a rich display of Max Beerbohm cartoons.

In the north-west corner of the quadrangle is a passage through which we reach the door of the chapel in the south transept. It is the first and the largest of college chapels. The choir was begun in 1290 and finished in 1294. The glass is in the main of the same period and particularly worthy of attention, as is also the remarkably skilful and intricate tracery of the east window. The lectern is of exquisitely spun brass of c. 1500. Three of the five arches of the screen (1671) designed by Sir Christopher Wren were set up in the crossing in 1960. There is exhilaration not only in the lively arches of the crossing, 1330, at the base of the bell-tower, which was finished in 1450 and contains eight bells, 1680, but also in the crystalline beauty of the transepts. They

7. Merton College: fifteenth-century relief over gateway; the library

8. Botanic Garden,
Magdalen Bridge,
and Magdalen College tower

9. Entrance to the
Examination Schools

are in the Perpendicular style, the south transept being built first, in 1367, and the north in 1416–24. The nave—the arches for which, and for its side aisles, are plainly discernible in the west wall—was never needed and never built. It is interesting to note that the glazing of the great west window cost £10. The glass in the ante-chapel windows is fifteenth-century.

Returning to the front quadrangle we may go through the Fitzjames gateway, built as part of new lodgings for the Warden in 1497, into the Fellows' quadrangle built by Warden Savile in 1608–10. A Yorkshireman, John Acroyd, was the mason and Thomas Holt, immediately afterwards employed at Wadham, did the timberwork. The whole is a beautiful and spacious example of late Gothic with a Renaissance feature in the middle of the south side. It set a new fashion in college building which was followed not only at Wadham, 1610–13, but also, as we have seen, at Oriel and University Colleges.

The Grove Buildings, at the south-west corner of the College, were built in 1864 by William Butterfield. They were so ugly that they were reconstructed in 1930, the top floor being removed in order to restore a balance with the rest of the College.

In 1905–10 the picturesque buildings of St. Alban Hall, which had been incorporated in Merton, were replaced by Champneys's routine quadrangle. He also built the grandiose Warden's Lodging on the other side of the street. This now accommodates the Science and Law libraries, three bachelor Fellows and some senior scholars, and the Warden has a new house facing westwards down Merton Street.

The beauties of Merton garden should not be missed. Its terrace stands above the southern line of the old city wall and overlooks the quiet expanse of Christ Church Meadow. From the Meadow there is a lovely view of the College.

Famous men: Thomas Bradwardine, Archbishop of Canterbury; Sir Thomas Bodley (Fellow); Anthony à Wood; Sir Richard Steele; William Harvey; Mandell Creighton, Bishop of London; Lord Randolph Churchill; Lord Halsbury (Lord Chancellor); Sir Max Beerbohm; T. S. Eliot, O.M.

Behind the houses opposite Merton is the tennis court, for Royal Tennis. Built in 1595, it was rebuilt in 1798. Edward VII played in it as Prince of Wales. The game has been played in Oxford since before 1450.

From Merton we may go on past the new History Faculty Library on our left and some nice old houses. Magdalen tower is in front of us. On the right, at the end of Merton garden are the remains of an old bastion of the city wall. Round the corner we see the eastward court of the Examination Schools (see p. 47).

The Eastgate Hotel marks the site of the old East Gate of the city, which was removed in 1771. We turn right, into 'the High' and just beyond Rose Lane, which leads into Christ Church Meadow and to the Cherwell walks, we come to

THE BOTANIC GARDEN

THE Botanic Garden, originally known as the Physick Garden because it was founded with special reference to the Faculty of Medicine, stands on the site of the former Jews' cemetery beside the Cherwell. The land was given by Henry Danvers, Earl of Danby, in 1621. It is a square enclosed by a lofty stone wall of the seventeenth century and the principal entrance, facing Magdalen College, is a handsome baroque gateway with pediment. Over the arch is a bust of Danby and in niches at the sides are statues of Charles I and Charles II. The first gardener was a German, Jacob Bobart from Brunswick, who collected 3,000 different sorts of plants. He was succeeded in 1669 by Robert Morison, who had been Physician to the Duke of Orléans and who was made Professor of Botany. From this garden there has spread all over England the yellow Oxford Ragwort (*Senecio squalida*) first grown here by Bobart from seeds collected on the slopes of Mt. Etna and sent to him.

Though small, the garden combines great beauty with efficiency. It has been extended beyond its wall to the south and the glass houses, last rebuilt in 1968–70, stand between the east wall and the river.

Crossing Magdalen Bridge, a pleasant, balustraded eighteenth-century structure, somewhat spoiled by successive widenings, we come to 'The Plain'. Here stood until 1828 old St. Clement's Church where J. H. Newman held his first curacy.

To the right are the grounds and buildings of Magdalen College School and beyond them, down Cowley Place, is

ST. HILDA'S COLLEGE

Founded 1893. *Present strength*: The Principal; 23 Fellows; 5 Research Fellows; 11 lecturers; 21 scholars; 22 exhibitioners; 319 other members receiving tuition or supervision.

 ST. HILDA'S was the fourth of the women's colleges. The founder, Miss Dorothea Beale, LL.D., Principal of a famous girls' school, Cheltenham Ladies' College, bought for her purpose Cowley House, which had been built in 1775 by Dr. Humphrey Sibthorpe, then Professor of Botany. It was beautifully situated on the banks of the Cherwell, by Milham Ford, and though it is the only college east of the river, it combines centrality with great quietude.

Called after St. Hilda of Whitby, it was opened with seven students in November 1893, six of the seven coming from Cheltenham. The house has been extended twice and neighbouring properties bought. After the First World War numbers reached 100 and in 1926 the College was incorporated by Royal Charter. In 1934 the Burrows Building, named after the two earliest Principals, was erected and since 1954 further extensions include the Sacher wing, the Wolfson Building, and the unusual but attractive Garden Building. There is a fine library.

Well-known members: D. K. Broster, Mrs. Cecil Woodham-Smith, Mrs. Chatterjee, Dame Helen Gardner, D.B.E.

If we turn right from St. Hilda's, down Iffley Road, passing on our right the University Athletics and Rugby

Football Grounds and the University Gymnasium (1966), we come on another Permanent Private Hall, accorded that status in 1957, namely,

GREYFRIARS

Present strength: The Warden; 4 tutors; 20 commoners.

 FROM early in the thirteenth century both Dominicans and Franciscans were powerful elements in the University and contributed some of its most eminent members, but their convents were dissolved in 1538 and their buildings disappeared. In 1910 the Franciscans returned to Oxford and since 1919 have occupied buildings in the Iffley Road. In 1957 they were given their present status. Formerly such of their members as were matriculated had joined St. Catherine's Society. Thus there are now three Roman Catholic Private Halls in the University.

The buildings, which include a large church, are of flint with red sandstone dressings, architecturally aliens in Oxford.

A little nearer to Magdalen Bridge and on the other side of the road are the Church and Mission House of the well-known *Cowley Fathers* (Society of St. John the Evangelist), founded by the Rev. R. M. Benson in 1865 'for the cultivation of a life dedicated to God according to the principles of Poverty, Chastity and Obedience'. They are an Anglican order and have branch houses in South Africa, the United States, Canada, and Japan. The church was completed in 1896.

Marston Street will take us into Cowley Road. Turning left we may walk to Dawson Street on our right and this will bring us into St. Clement's. Behind York Place there is the new building, designed by James Stirling, for The Queen's College. It stands on the bank of the Cherwell, looking across the meadows to Magdalen.

Encased in dull red tiles, it is like an inverted pyramid

with five sides of varying length and its nose buried in the ground. It is supported by six concrete struts. Three narrow bands of glass run round the building and there are twin towers at the south-east corner. There is a wider line of glass at the top, with parapet and balcony.

From the north, or inner side, we see what looks like a concave cascade of glass like a frozen Niagara descending to a platform covering common and breakfast rooms, and with stepped seats in its western angle. Is there any other building like it?

Coming back to Magdalen Bridge we pass on our right the latest buildings of Magdalen College and are aware of three branches of the ever-divisive Cherwell and its green water-meadows, but dominating the scene is Magdalen's exquisitely graceful bell-tower. James I described it as 'the most absolute building in Oxford' and someone else has likened it to a lily, a long stalk with the flower at the top.

MAGDALEN COLLEGE

Founded 1458. *Present strength*: The President; 59 Fellows; 7 lecturers; 2 Senior Demies; 25 Demies, 18 scholars, 41 exhibitioners; an organist, 12 clerks, 16 academical choristers; 295 B.A.s and commoners. *Buildings*: Lodge gateway, 1884; wall surrounding College site and grove and including tower at St. Cross and Longwall Street corner, 1467–73; St. John's Hospital *nucleus*, thirteenth-century; kitchen, thirteenth- or early-fourteenth-century; chapel, 1474–5; hall and cloister quadrangle, 1475; Founder's Tower, 1485–8; Muniment Tower, 1487–8; bell-tower, 1492–1509; west range, incorporating and extending St. John's Hospital, sixteenth-century; Grammar Hall, 1614; New Buildings, 1733; West's Building (beyond kitchen), 1783; north front of cloister rebuilt 1824; new (undergraduate) library, 1851; St. Swithun's quadrangle, 1880–4; President's Lodging rebuilt 1886–8; Long Wall quadrangle, 1931; Cherwell building, 1962–3.

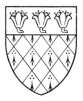 To Magdalen (pronounced *Maudlin*) we owe an immeasurable debt for two things in particular. One is the loveliness of the bell-tower and the other is the heroic resistance offered at a vital time to the tyranny of King James II.

The founder, William of Waynflete, was a New College man who was successively

Headmaster of Winchester, Headmaster and then Provost of Eton, and later Bishop of Winchester and Lord Chancellor of England. He began by setting up a hall, dedicated to St. Mary Magdalene, on a site in the High Street just west of the present Examination Schools, but in 1457 Henry VI granted him the site and buildings of St. John's Hospital beyond the East Gate, and so the hall was dissolved and the College was established. Just as New College was an advance on Merton, so Magdalen was an advance on New College, and it was immediately the wealthiest foundation in the University. As Macaulay says in his *History of England*: 'At the time of the general visitation in the reign of Henry VIII the revenues were far larger than those of any similar institution in the realm, larger by nearly one-half than those of the magnificent foundation of Henry VI at Cambridge, and considerably more than twice as large as those which William of Wykeham had settled on his college in Oxford.' It is still one of the three richest colleges in Oxford.

Waynflete provided for a President, forty Fellows, thirty scholars (called *demies* because they had half the allowance of a Fellow), four chaplain-priests, eight clerks, sixteen choristers, and a master and an usher for a grammar school (which is still continued as Magdalen College School, where, with many other boys, the boys of the choir are educated). The biggest innovation was the allotting of rooms for twenty high-born youths who should pay for enjoying the privileges of the foundation. These soon became a characteristic element in all colleges and were known as 'gentlemen commoners' or 'noblemen' and wore specially braided silk gowns with, in the case of noblemen, gold tufts to their caps.

Knowledge of plain-song and a good grounding in grammar were qualifications for election to Demyships and the wide curriculum included, besides Latin and Greek, Logic, Sophistry, Theology, Natural and Moral Philosophy, Mathematics and Astronomy and, for a limited number of Fellows, Canon and Civil Law and Medicine. Latin had to be spoken. No hounds, hawks, cards, dice, or extravagant dress were allowed. The President could be absent as he pleased, but

Fellows could be away for only sixty days in the year and Demies, thirty. There was a fire in hall on saints' days.

Waynflete lived to see his buildings all but complete except for the bell-tower and entertained both Edward IV and Richard III in them. He died in 1486. Henry VII visited the College twice and Arthur, Prince of Wales, three times. There is a pathetic memorial of the latter in the tapestry which hangs in the royal rooms in the Founder's Tower and depicts his marriage with the ill-fated Catherine of Aragon.

Wolsey was a Fellow of the College from *c*. 1491 till 1501.

The chapel suffered much damage in the Edwardian reformation when the figures of the reredos were destroyed and the plate and vestments were sold for a twentieth of their value. The College continued to be strongly Puritan until the time of Charles I, when it rallied, with the rest of the University, to his cause and gave him nearly all its silver, more than any other college, in 1642. In 1646 the Presbyterians took away the Founder's crosier and mitre and these were never recovered. His ceremonial stockings and buskins, however, are preserved in the library, and the medieval cope exhibited in the ante-chapel probably belonged to him. Under the Parliamentary visitation in 1647, President Oliver and twenty-eight Fellows were removed; only six submitted. But this staunch loyalty to the Stuarts was ill requited. When President Clerke died in 1687 James II ordered the Fellows to elect a Roman Catholic, Anthony Farmer, whose vicious life was notorious and who had been expelled from Cambridge. Farmer was disqualified not only by his evil reputation but also by the fact that he had never been a Fellow of either Magdalen or New College, as the statutes required. The College respectfully begged the King to excuse them and waited as long as the statutes allowed in the hope that James might make a more suitable nomination. When none came they elected John Hough whom the Visitor at once admitted to office. This infuriated the King, who called the Fellows before the Court of High Commission, and now ordered them to elect Samuel Parker, Bishop of Oxford, who was also unqualified. The Fellows pointed out that there was no vacancy, Hough having been properly elected and admitted. James then came to Oxford and sent for them to come to the Deanery at Christ Church, where he furiously rated them as they knelt before him and told them that unless they did as he bade them, he would not only turn them out but would bar them for ever from any preferment in the Church; that is to say he would deprive them of all means of livelihood. Only three Fellows submitted to him and less than half the Demies, but the contest had raised such feeling that a public subscription was raised to help the ejected, and the King's own daughter, Mary, gave £200. Parker was installed by proxy and before the end of the year twelve Roman Catholic Fellows had been appointed. Parker died in March and was succeeded by one Giffard, a Roman Catholic bishop and chaplain to the King. But the popular enthusiasm aroused by the acquittal of the Seven Bishops in June, the dismay caused by the birth of the Old Pretender, and the movement afoot to put William of Orange on the throne, caused James to begin, too late, to retreat. He permitted the restoration of Hough and the expelled Fellows on 25 October 1688, a day ever after celebrated at Magdalen as Restoration Day. Two months later his exile began and the reign of Stuart kings had ended.

Despite the 'Golden Election' of 1689 when, among the Demies admitted were Joseph Addison and Henry Sacheverell, Magdalen played no great part in Oxford history during the next two centuries. Its wealth and torpor and the idleness of the Fellows were denounced by the youthful Gibbon, who spent fourteen months there in 1752–3.

Perhaps the most remarkable feature of Magdalen's history in this period was the reign of Martin Routh. He was a Demy in 1771, a Fellow in 1775, and President from 1791 till he died, all but 100 years old, in 1854. He was said to have been the last Englishman outside the legal profession to wear a wig. The wig is in the library. It was in his day, 1799, that the chains were removed from the library books.

Magdalen has always been famed for its music in chapel

and it may be pertinent to note that Sir John Stainer was organist from 1859 to 1872 and Sir Walter Parratt from 1872 till 1908.

On entering the College we have, to our right, the adapted buildings of St. John's Hospital and, in the corner, is the open-air pulpit from which until 1958 a sermon was preached to the University every St. John Baptist's Day, 24 June; though now it is usually delivered on the nearest Sunday.

The other buildings of this quadrangle are the ante-chapel, the Muniment Tower, the Founder's Tower, with richly carved bay windows and the President's Lodging. Then, standing by itself is the Grammar Hall, which is not as old as it looks (1614 rebuilt in 1828) and is now used as undergraduates' sets of rooms; and, on our left, St. Swithun's quadrangle (1880–4) beyond which are the Longwall Buildings, magnificently fitted in oak.

If we go under the Muniment Tower we find irnmediately to our right the door into the chapel or, rather, the ante-chapel, for William of Waynflete followed the T-shaped plan which New College adopted from Merton and which All Souls had used thirty years before in 1442. The architectural form of the chapel is satisfying and beautiful: its proportions are good and the arches of the ante-chapel are particularly graceful, but in general the fittings are poor. The reredos is a modern restoration of what was destroyed at the Reformation; the opulent stalls date from *c.* 1830, when the original ones were relegated to the ante-chapel; the present windows, ascribed to Richard Greenbury and done in a sepia tint, date from 1632. The lectern, given by President Frewen in 1633, is good. The altar picture, *The Bearing of the Cross*, is of the Seville school (*c.* 1660). In the little chantry chapel is the tomb of the Founder's father, Richard Patten: its date is about 1450 and it was removed from All Saints' Church, Wainfleet, when that was pulled down in 1809.

Coming out of the chapel we should go on into the cloister and turn left. There is beautiful vaulting under the Founder's Tower. If we continue into the north side of the cloister we get a fine view of the hall and chapel with the bell-tower behind them. Then we should turn round and slip through a passage which will bring us out to the lawns in front of the New Building, 1733. There were many schemes to turn Oxford into a sort of Dresden at about that time. Queen's had just pulled down its medieval buildings and erected the colonnades and pediments and cupolas we see there now. Peckwater had just been built at Christ Church; Trinity Chapel dates from 1691; Worcester was shortly to adopt a classical shape, and the Radcliffe Camera was soon to come; Corpus had built their Fellows' Building by 1712. There are other examples—All Saints' Church, 1707, is one, Christ Church library another. There was a grandiose scheme to turn Brasenose into something like the Vatican City and if the architects had had their way nothing of the Magdalen we see would have survived except the chapel, hall, and bell-tower. Originally the New Building was to be the north side of a new quadrangle and not till 1824 was this scheme abandoned and the end wings finished. As it is, the gracious eighteenth-century building with its long Georgian windows, parapet, and central pediment, looks across the grass to the reconstructed fifteenth-century quadrangle of the Founder, and very good neighbours they are, each setting the other off by contrast.

The New Building stands on the edge of the Grove with its lovely elms and herd of deer. To the east are the water-meadows, surrounded by the branches of the Cherwell and Addison's Walk, named after the poet and statesman of Queen Anne's day and *Spectator* fame, the creator of Sir Roger de Coverley. The path is a fairyland of flowers in March and the far end of the meadow is full of fritillaries in April. No other college has such extensive grounds as Magdalen, more than 100 acres.

Returning from the bridge over the river, we may go south towards the gabled group of buildings by the kitchen, which is certainly older than the College and probably belonged to the Hospital of St. John. If we are permitted to enter we shall see the old spits as at Christ Church and the louvre in the middle of the roof for the escape of the smoke.

10. St. Edmund Hall: quadrangle; library and entrance to chapel

11. The High Street with The Queen's College, All Souls College, and St. Mary's Church

12. The Queen's College: library

In the south-east corner of the cloister are the steps up to the hall. The Jacobean screen is the finest in Oxford, *c.* 1600; the beautiful linen-fold panelling of the rest of the hall is nearly a hundred years older. Of particular note are the carved panels in the middle of the wall over the High Table. In the centre is Henry VIII and above and below him are incidents in the life of St. Mary Magdalene, with the date 1541. The noble oriel window contains seventeenth-century portraits of Charles I and Henrietta Maria and sixteenth-century coats of arms of contemporary bishops. There are pictures of Reginald Pole, d. 1558, the last Roman Catholic Archbishop of Canterbury; Henry, Prince of Wales; Prince Rupert, Charles I's great cavalry leader; and President Routh.

If we turn left on descending the stairs and then left again we shall come into the Chaplains' quadrangle and so to the foot of the bell-tower, on the top of which a Latin hymn is sung at 6 a.m. on May morning. After the singing the bells crash out and the tower sways with the din of them. They are the sweetest of the many Oxford peals. The ten bells are of various dates from early in the fifteenth century onwards to 1712.

The new Waynflete building is at the east end of Magdalen bridge.

Famous men: Richard Foxe, Bishop of Winchester; Cardinal Wolsey; Cardinal Pole; John Colet; John Lyly; Sir Thomas Bodley; John Hampden; Joseph Addison; William Collins, the poet; Henry Sacheverell; Edward Gibbon; John Conington; Roundell Palmer, 1st Earl of Selborne; Charles Reade; Goldwin Smith; Oscar Wilde; Sir Robert Robinson, O.M. (Fellow); Sir Peter Medawar (Nobel Prize Winner); Howard Walter, 1st Baron Florey, P.R.S.

If on leaving Magdalen we turn back up the High Street we pass, on our left, the Rose Lane entrance into Christ Church Meadow, with its beautiful walks along the banks of Cherwell and Thames, and on our right, Longwall, so called because it is a street that runs along outside the city wall. Soon we are at the point where the East Gate stood till its removal in 1771 and just beyond, on the left, are the EXAMINATION SCHOOLS.

These were designed by Sir Thomas Jackson, R.A., in the Elizabethan style of Kirby Hall, Northamptonshire, and were opened in 1882. They were needed to replace the Old Schools which were absorbed into the Bodleian Library and they stand on the site of the Angel Inn. They are built of Clipsham stone which has worn well. The carvings over the main entrance depicting the viva voce examination and the degree ceremony are particularly worth notice.

To these spacious rooms undergraduates flock for lectures during term, but at the beginning of June they become the scene of 'Final Schools', that is, of the degree examinations. For three successive weeks over two thousand candidates spend six days working their papers, and by the end of July most of them will have returned for a brief spell to be examined viva voce upon their written answers. As soon as the last viva in any School is finished the Class List is published on the boards in the entrance hall. Many a man's future depends on where his name occurs.

All undergraduates wear gowns for lectures, but for examinations men must wear dark suits ('subfusc') as well, with white bow ties and black shoes, and must wear or carry their mortar boards; women must wear dark skirts, white blouses with black ties, stockings, and shoes. Graduates undergoing examination wear the hood of their degree. Examiners and invigilators similarly wear full academic dress.

The Examination Schools are not the only place for lectures. Lectures, open to members of the University, are given in many University buildings and in all colleges, quite often in college halls.

A little farther up the High, on the right, is Queen's Lane and a few yards up the lane is

ST. EDMUND HALL

Opened in the thirteenth century. *Present strength*: The Principal; 32 Fellows; 1 Research Fellow; 10 lecturers; 45 scholars; 3 senior scholars; 44 exhibitioners; 334 other members receiving tuition or supervision. *Buildings*: hall, c. 1660; chapel and library, 1680; east half of north range, late sixteenth-century; west half, c. 1741; a large fire-place in the Junior Common Room is fifteenth-century; existing south range is largely modern and was completed in 1934; new building, 1969.

 ST. EDMUND HALL, described by the late C. R. L. Fletcher in 1915 as 'a tiny foundation whose normal complement of men seldom reaches thirty'—actually it was forty in 1913— is interesting as the only one of the medieval halls to survive till our own day. Since 1957, however, it has become a college like the rest, though it keeps its old designation.

The first written mention of it is in a rent roll of Oseney Abbey of 1317, but we know that the Abbey owned it from 1270 and it was pretty certainly a recognized hall before that. It is traditionally held that St. Edmund of Abingdon lived here when he was lecturing in Oxford and that he built the little chapel on the north side of the chancel of St. Peter-in-the-East.

The Hall was ruled by its own Principals who were admitted by the Chancellor and paid their rent to the Abbey until the Dissolution in 1539. Then, after an interlude of eighteen years, it was bought by Queen's and from 1557 till 1937 Queen's appointed the Principals from her own Fellows. It was almost a miracle that the Hall avoided absorption by its greater neighbour, but in 1937 it became independent; the Principal ceased to be an autocrat and shared the government with his Vice-Principal and tutors, thereafter called Fellows.

It is interesting that in 1852 the Royal Commission on the University reported that despite its lack of endowment the Hall was then one of the cheapest places of education in Oxford. It was stated that the highest undergraduate bills there in 1849 had amounted to only £80. 0s. 5d. for the year and the lowest to £60. 18s. 7d. There were twenty-five undergraduates in residence. At Pembroke the total cost of a degree course was estimated at £370 on an average: at Merton costs were £150 a year, and at University College £100; but this was for frugal men.[1]

The Hall has grown to its present eminence partly through the stimulus of two post-war periods and partly through the personality of its last two Principals. No one could now call it either tiny or insignificant, whether in the Schools, on the games field, or on the river.

The somewhat dull exterior holds no hint of the charm of the quadrangle that opens out at the end of the passage. To the immediate left is the small former hall, then the delightful north range with its mullioned windows, and the painted sundial, and in front, beyond the well-head, the classical ante-chapel with the old library above and chapel beyond it. The chapel has beautiful stalls *c.* 1682. The screen is of oak on the west face and cedar on the east. The altar-piece, *Supper at Emmaus*, is by Mr. Ceri Richards (1958).

The old library is long and narrow with shelves lining the walls. Half-way up them runs a gallery with seventeenth-century balusters. It was probably the first library to be built on the wall system, i.e. instead of having cubicles, and the last to be chained. The chains were removed in 1760.

Going on past the chapel we come into a new world, squeezed between New College garden and the High, where the architect, Gilbert Howes, has contrived to place relatively enormous buildings in no space without offending important neighbours except that one range, the western one (Kelly) is a storey too high and hurts the skyline. With its sharp pointed gables it is like a white Rothenburg on stilts. There is a roof garden over the J.C.R., a stylish dining hall given by Sir Isaac Wolfson, and a Senior Common Room. The Besse building fronts the High.

Famous men: Thomas Hearne, diarist and gossip; Sir Richard Blackmore, an eminent physician and indifferent poet; John Oldham, poet; White Kennett, Bishop of Peterborough; John Methuen, Lord Chancellor of Ireland, author of the Methuen Treaty with Portugal (1704); Sir John Stainer.

[1] Mallet, op. cit. iii. 305–6.

Next to St. Edmund Hall is the ancient Church of ST. PETER-IN-THE-EAST, now the College library. There are two churches of St. Peter, east and west, the other being St. Peter-le-Bailey,[1] in the castle precincts, and there were two of St. Michael, one at the North Gate and one at the South, the four making a diamond-shaped pattern on the map. St. Michael-at-the-South-Gate was pulled down to make room for Christ Church.

Until 1827 University afternoon sermons were preached at this St. Peter's during Lent and the numbers attending them were so great that it was necessary to put a gallery up at the west end, but this was later removed.

The fourteenth-century tower is plain and tapers towards the top where there is a carved parapet. There were eight bells and a sanctus. The east end is distinguished by the 'candle-snuffer' tops to the square Norman buttresses and by the typical Norman work below the parapet of the chancel; the south-west door is an excellent example of twelfth-century work, though the porch which protects it is fifteenth-century. The chancel, c. 1140, is wide and well-proportioned. The chapel, 1230–40, to the north of it was probably built by St. Edmund of Abingdon for his own scholars, and the crypt below the chancel, now reached only from the outside, is the most exciting feature of all. It is 36 ft. × 21 ft. and has eight independent pillars with carved capitals and Norman windows. Formerly there were two staircases to the chancel in the north and south walls and two passages and stairs to the nave from the west wall, with a vaulted chamber between them.

It is sad when any great church ceases to be used for worship, but the next best use is as a library, and 'Teddy Hall' has made a fine one here, full of life and colour, a splendid room to work in.

On the opposite side of the lane is

[1] Now the chapel of St. Peter's College.

THE QUEEN'S COLLEGE

Founded 1341. *Present strength*: The Provost; 34 Fellows; 5 travelling Fellows; 5 lecturers; 66 scholars; 4 senior scholars; 66 exhibitioners; 205 other members receiving tuition or supervision. *Buildings*: entrance and High Street front, 1733–5; chapel, 1714–19; hall, 1714–15; library, 1692–5; first quadrangle, 1709–60; second quadrangle, 1672–1707; new quadrangle, 1969–70.

 FROM the fourteenth century till 1751 the main entrance to Queen's lay through a gabled gatehouse opposite St. Edmund Hall. It led into a quadrangle which had the chapel and ante-chapel on the south, the Provost's Lodging and hall on the west, and kitchen and chambers on the north and east sides. The library was tucked away beyond the ante-chapel in the south-west corner of the site. The college was cut off from the High Street by a row of shops and their gardens. The buildings had the appearance of being rather haphazard and not very grand. This was, no doubt, due to the fact that the Founder's ambitions were greater than his financial capacity.

Robert de Eglesfield, a native of Cumberland and chaplain to Queen Philippa, wife of Edward III, founded the College, under the patronage of his mistress in 1341. There were to be a Provost and twelve scholars, representing Our Lord and his Apostles, who were to study Theology; thirteen chaplains; seventy-two 'poor boys' or 'disciples', some of whom were to constitute the choir; and every day pea soup was to be served to the indigent at the gate. The statutes provided that the course in Theology should last for eighteen years; that the Fellows should wear red gowns in hall to commemorate Christ's death; and that they should be summoned to dinner by trumpet. This last provision is the only one which, in term time, is still observed, but on feast nights, in the centre of the High Table, there is still the Founder's magnificent Loving Cup, an auroch's[1] horn mounted with eagle's feet and bands of silver gilt. From Eglesfield's day till now the College has enjoyed the patronage of the Queens Consort of England. This has often been

[1] *V.C.H. Oxfordshire*, iii. 134.

of great advantage. It was probably through Queen Philippa's influence that Edward III gave to the College the Wardenship of St. Julian's Hospital or God's House in Southampton, an endowment which still makes a large contribution to the College's revenues.

To ease its early poverty, when the income was never enough to maintain its full strength of Fellows and 'poor boys' and there was plenty of room to spare, the College admitted paying guests or *commensales* and thus acquired some of the most famous names in its roll: John Wyclif, Cardinal Henry Beaufort, and his nephews Henry V and Richard Courtenay, Chancellor of the University and Bishop of Norwich. The way in which the number of these non-foundationers grew is shown by the fact that there were 14 such *commoners* in 1535, 70 in 1581, and 194 in 1612.[1] The Fellows increased their meagre stipends by acting as their tutors. The foundation, i.e. Fellows and scholars, was elected largely from the counties of Cumberland and Westmorland until the principle of open competition was applied in the reforms of the nineteenth century. It is because it was usually too far for these northerners to go home for the Christmas Vacation that Queen's became famous for its Boar's Head procession and dinner on Christmas Day and its Needle and Thread feast on New Year's Day. On this occasion the Bursar gives each guest a needle and thread, saying: 'Take this and be thrifty.' The origin of the ceremony is said to be a pun on Eglesfield's name (*aiguille et fil*).

Architecturally Queen's began to be transformed when Sir Joseph Williamson, a 'poor boy' who rose to be Secretary of State in 1674, paid for a new block to be built along Queen's Lane and to the north of the old buildings in 1672. Williamson touched off a resolution to have all things new. Provost Halton built the beautiful library in 1692–5 to house Bishop Barlow's bequest of books. The design has been attributed to Dean Aldrich, and the original library on the upper floor is one of the finest rooms in Oxford. To begin with the eastern half of the ground floor was an open loggia.

[1] *V.C.H. Oxfordshire*, iii. 134.

53

This north quadrangle was completed by the building of the north range in 1707. Two years later the front quadrangle, as we see it, was begun. The hall was finished in 1715 and the chapel was consecrated in 1719. Most of the glass in the new chapel was taken from the old: the two west windows on each side date from 1518 and the rest, except the east window (1715) are by Abraham van Linge, 1635. The lectern, 1653, also belonged to the old chapel. The fine candelabra were given in 1721. The *Ascension* on the ceiling over the apse was painted by Sir James Thornhill. The tomb of the Founder is in the crypt.

Lack of funds prevented the completion of the front quadrangle until 1760. Queen Caroline gave £1,000 in 1733 and bequeathed another £1,000 in 1737, thus earning for herself a statue under the cupola at the gate. The original gatehouse on Queen's Lane stood until 1757. Even in 1726 and before the scheme was finished Daniel Defoe described Queen's as 'without comparison the most Beautiful College in the University'. Certainly it is a remarkable and splendid example of spacious eighteenth-century architecture and unique among Oxford and Cambridge colleges.

Visitors who have the time should go along the walled passage which runs westwards from the south of the library to the old College brewery, now, alas, disused, and turn left into Nunn's Garden. There they will find a picturesque quietude behind the old houses of the High and within a stone's throw of roaring traffic. One of these old houses, Drawda Hall, still bears the name of William of Drogheda, who taught in Oxford in the thirteenth century.

In 1959 a new Provost's Lodging was built on the site of the old stable yard in Queen's Lane: it is in a tactful mixture of styles, harmonizing well with the rest of the College.

Reference to Queen's latest building was made on p. 40. In 1969–70 the College built a new quadrangle on the other side of Queen's Lane between the High and St. Edmund Hall. Great care was taken by the architect, Mr. Marshall Sisson, to preserve the seventeenth- and eighteenth-century fronts of the shops facing the street and even the shops have been preserved, while rooms for fifty undergraduates and

. University College:
teway to the Radcliffe
adrangle

apel screen

14. All Souls College: north quadrangle. Beyond are New College on the left and The Queen's College on the right

two fellows have been provided; an architectural triumph
blending the most modern with the elegance of a former age.

Famous men: Edmund Halley; Henry Compton, Bishop of London; Thomas
Middleton; William Wycherley; Thomas Tickell; Joseph Addison; Jeremy
Bentham; William Thomson, Archbishop of York; Walter Pater; A. H.
Sayce, the Orientalist. Archbishop William Temple (Fellow); Lord Florey
(Provost).

On the opposite side of the High and a little farther up
are the curved front and two gate-towers of

UNIVERSITY COLLEGE

Founded 1249. *Present strength*: The Master; 38 Fellows; 6 Research Fellows;
2 travelling Fellows; 8 lecturers; 55 scholars; 41 exhibitioners; 321 other
members receiving tuition or supervision. *Buildings*: Gatehouse, 1638;
chapel, 1666; hall, 1656, extended 1904; library, 1861; first quadrangle,
1634–75; second quadrangle, 1716–19; Master's Lodging, 1879; Shelley
Memorial, 1894; Durham Building, 1903; Goodhart quadrangle, 1962.

ALTHOUGH the statutes of University College (commonly called *Univ.*) date from about
1280, sixteen years later than the first statutes
of Merton, the College can claim an earlier
origin than either Merton or Balliol, since the
money for its foundation was left to the University by William of Durham in 1249. The
reason why it used to take precedence of all other colleges
in the *University Calendar*, however, is that from the late
fourteenth century it was widely believed to have been
founded by King Alfred, a view which was confirmed by
the Court of King's Bench in 1727, when a disputed election
to the Mastership of the College necessitated a legal deci-
sion on whether the Crown or the University was the
College's Visitor.

The Founder's object was that the University should set
up a college of ten, eleven, or twelve Masters of Arts to
study Theology. All the early colleges were for postgraduate
study: undergraduates, whether scholars or commoners
(paying members), came later.

With the money, 310 marks, that is to say, about £200 (1 mark = 13s. 4d. = 67np), the University bought property, probably on the north-east corner of Brasenose, but by 1280 the sum had shrunk and thus the community began with only 'four Masters, well-lettered and well-conducted'. They each got fifty shillings yearly, except that the bursar got an extra five and the senior among them, who also acted as Head and chaplain, also got a little extra after 1292. For many years they were subject to the oversight of the University and not till the middle of the fourteenth century did they become substantially independent.

The present site of the College was acquired by two purchases made in 1332 and 1336, and as time went on the College grew in both directions along the High Street and also in depth to Kybald Street southwards. It also received benefactions in the way of Fellowships and scholarships from Walter Skirlaw, Bishop of Durham (d. 1405); Henry, second Earl of Northumberland (son of the famous Hotspur) (1394–1455); and Sir Simon Bennett, Bt. (d. 1631). Dr. John Radcliffe, physician to William III and Queen Anne, a considerable benefactor, left £5,000 to build the second quadrangle and other money for travelling Fellowships.

Obadiah Walker, Master 1676–89, became a Roman Catholic and set up his own 'Mass-house' within the College, as well as that statue of James II which still stands in the south side of the gate-tower, but when James was overthrown Walker fell too. Perhaps its most distinguished epoch began about 1765 when among the Fellows were Sir Robert Chambers, the Indian judge, who was Vinerian Professor of English Law; William Scott, later the first Lord Stowell; his brother John, who became Lord Chancellor and first Earl of Eldon; and the Orientalist, Sir William Jones. All of these were intimates of the great Dr. Johnson, who often stayed with them, and would drink three bottles of port at a sitting without feeling any the worse for it. In 1811 the College authorities showed some lack of tact when they expelled Shelley and his friend Hogg for publishing a pamphlet on *The Necessity of Atheism*.

We do not know much about the original buildings of the

College. It had its own chapel from about 1400 and a new hall and kitchen were built in 1448–9. We know from Bereblock's sketch of 1566 that the buildings then formed a quadrangle and Anthony à Wood has left us a revealing sketch of the old chapel and library in its south-west corner. Nothing that we see now, however, is earlier than the seventeenth century. Demolition and rebuilding were begun in 1634 and continued till 1677. The style adopted was that late Gothic already employed at Wadham and Oriel, only it is not quite so bold or successful. The curved front on the High is well managed, but the Gothic 'frontispiece' between hall and chapel, 1802, is not so attractive as its rather fussy Renaissance predecessor which we see in Loggan's print of 1675. The statue over the main gate, facing the High, is of Queen Anne (1709) and the statues on the tower of the Radcliffe quadrangle are of Queen Mary II and of Radcliffe himself (1719). The chapel suffered from severe handling by Gilbert Scott in 1862. His timber roof is graceless and his gothicizing of the east end has been mitigated by Sir Michael Sadler's restoration of the seventeenth-century carved reredos. The seventeenth-century stalls and screen are good and some of the fine carving of the latter may well be by the same hand as worked on that in Trinity Chapel. Abraham van Linge's glass (1641–2) is notable and so is Flaxman's monument to Sir William Jones in the ante-chapel.

The hall is dull and its proportions were spoiled when it was lengthened in 1904, but there are some interesting portraits, including a 'conversation piece' of the Cecil family, showing the third Marquess of Salisbury with his three sons—Lord Cecil of Chelwood, Lord Quickswood, and the Bishop of Exeter.

The Shelley Memorial will be found in the near right-hand corner of the first quadrangle. It is by Onslow Ford and shows the poet as he lay drowned on the Pisan shore.

There are fine examples of sixteenth- and seventeenth-century panelling and carving in the Summer Common Room and in the first- and second-floor rooms of No. 90 High Street, which was incorporated with the College in 1905.

The modern library was designed by Scott; its predecessor, behind the hall, has been turned into a beautiful room by Dr. A. L. Goodhart, Hon. K.B.E. (Master, 1951–63). The latest building, designed by Professor Matthew of Edinburgh and Mr. Johnson-Marshall, is between the Master's Lodging and the Examination Schools and incorporates ·Logic Lane. It was opened in 1962, another munificent gift of Dr. Goodhart.

Famous men: John Tiptoft, Earl of Worcester; Lord Herbert of Cherbury; Dr. John Radcliffe; Sir Roger Newdigate, Bt.; Lord Hastings, Governor-General of India; Shelley; Robert, first Viscount Cecil of Chelwood; Clement Richard, first Earl Attlee; Dr. C. H. Dodd, C.H.

Crossing the High Street again, we come next to

ALL SOULS COLLEGE

Founded 1438. *Present strength*: The Warden; 65 Fellows; 16 Visiting Fellows; 2 readers and lecturers; 1 chaplain. There are no undergraduates. *Buildings*: gatehouse, 1438; chapel, 1442; hall, 1730; Codrington library, completed in 1756; front quadrangle, 1438–42; great quadrangle, 1714–34; Warden's Lodgings, 1704–6.

 UNTIL Nuffield and St. Antony's came into existence, All Souls was unique among Oxford and Cambridge colleges in that it alone had preserved the medieval habit of admitting only graduates. Since the four Bible Clerkships were suppressed in 1926 none but graduates, and those only of the highest academic distinction, have been elected to the foundation.

The College of All Souls of the Faithful Departed has been described as the greatest of all war memorials. It was dedicated particularly to those who had fallen in the Hundred Years War and was thus a chantry[1] as well as an academic society. It was founded by Henry Chichele (pronounced *Chitchely*), Archbishop of Canterbury, in 1437, and his King, Henry VI, acted as co-founder, though he was himself busy at the time with his own projected colleges at

[1] A chantry was a place of prayer for souls.

58

Eton and Cambridge. Endowments were provided by estates scattered about in nine different counties. Both in ground plan and in statutes Chichele followed the lines laid down at New College sixty years before, for Chichele was a New College man. The chapel contained numerous saintly relics, including a tooth of John the Baptist, and indulgences were granted to those who came and worshipped there. The library was richly furnished with manuscripts, among them a fine copy of Eusebius's *Ecclesiastical History*, the gift of the King, and the famous 'Amesbury' Psalter, but many were lost or discarded at the Reformation, when the chapel also was despoiled. In 1548 the figures in the splendid reredos and the rich altar-fittings were ripped out, in 1550 copes and vestments were sold and in 1551 the glorious colours of the choir hidden under whitewash. The organ was removed and has never been replaced. The Reformation did not much alter the composition of the College, and Warden Hovenden, who ruled from 1571 till 1614, was a wise administrator. None the less the society suffered from two evils which long continued. One was corrupt resignations, whereby Fellows sold their places to ill-qualified successors for prodigious sums, and the other was riotous and factious behaviour, the result of indiscipline within. On several occasions the Fellows had to be rebuked by the Visitor, the Archbishop of Canterbury, for their brawling and their potations. Some of these lapses were, in the seventeenth century, associated with the cult of the Mallard, a bird which according to tradition is supposed to have been found in a drain soon after the College was founded. Many constitutional changes, the result of Royal Commissions (which respected the essential character of the College), took place in the nineteenth and twentieth centuries. The College's wealth has increased, and its riches are magnificently deployed to serve scholarship of all cultures.

All Souls blossomed particularly during the Commonwealth. Warden Sheldon, afterwards Archbishop of Canterbury, and a few Fellows were expelled, but among those introduced were Christopher Wren, later Savilian Professor of Astronomy, and Thomas Sydenham, 'the most original

59

medical genius of his age',[1] both from Wadham. Whereas it has always been the privilege of Christ Church to entertain royalty when they visit Oxford it was at All Souls that Cromwell stayed whenever he visited the University as its Chancellor, 1651–8.

From that time the College has always recruited many of the best minds in Oxford and for many years an All Souls Fellowship has been regarded as the greatest academic distinction open to a young Oxonian. As it is possible in certain circumstances both to hold an All Souls Fellowship and pursue a career in the public service or at the Bar there is an unusually close link between the College and the great world outside. The learned Chichele Professor of Modern History, the late Sir Charles Oman, is reported to have said that if during the day he came up against a question he could not answer, there was no need for him to look the matter up, for he was sure to meet in the Common Room or at dinner someone who knew all about it.

Since 1966 the College has elected not less than twelve men every year for not more than two years each to Visiting Fellowships. All are distinguished scholars in their respective subjects, and they come from universities all over the world, even from behind the 'Iron Curtain'.

The College has a simple, domestic front and a modest gate-tower, built originally to house the Warden and the muniments. Its sculptures, facing the street, replace older ones, and are by Mr. W. C. H. King, 1939. The front quadrangle, virtually unaltered since it was finished in 1441, surprises by its neatness, its smallness, and the musk growing in the stones at the foot of the wall. The chapel is a graceful piece of fifteenth-century Perpendicular Gothic and its interior is one of the most impressive in Oxford. The four east windows of the ante-chapel are original glass; the massive seventeenth-century screen in black and gold, though alien in style, fits perfectly, a typical stroke of the genius of other days. The stalls, with their fine misericords, are original, but the marble floor displaced medieval tiles in the seventeenth century. Covering the east wall of the

[1] Mallet, op. cit. i. 378.

chapel, behind and above the altar, is the restored fifteenth-century reredos, but although most of its canopied niches and pedestals are original all the figures are modern. In 1664 the ruins of the first reredos were boarded up and a Last Judgement was painted over it—'too full of nakeds for a college chapel', said John Evelyn, but whether it was on account of the 'nakeds' or some other suggestiveness of the Last Day, the Fellows removed it in 1714. The reredos was then plastered up and Sir James Thornhill painted over it a picture of the resurrection of the Founder. Beneath it was added, in 1771, a baldacchino framing the picture *Noli me tangere* by Raphael Mengs. During some repairs in 1870 it was accidentally discovered that the canopies of the original reredos remained. The plaster was removed and new figures were carved at the cost of the sixth Earl Bathurst (1875). The result is extremely pleasing, far finer than the restorations at New College and Magdalen and the effect is heightened by the survival of a good deal of the medieval colouring.

On the first floor of the east side of the quadrangle is the old library, now a lecture room, with a fine plaster ceiling, 1598.

The first hall was at right angles to the chapel running northwards from its east end, but it was pulled down and the present hall erected in 1730. This was in connexion with schemes of reconstruction running in the mind of Dr. George Clarke, for many years M.P. for the University and a distinguished amateur architect, and with the munificent bequest by Sir Christopher Codrington of all his books and £6,000 for a new library. The result was the substitution of the present great quadrangle with its remarkable twin towers for the old cloister and burial ground. Hawksmoor,[1] associated with Wren in many of his greatest works, was the architect. There is no question of the magnificence of the Codrington Library, finished in 1756, the money for which was made out of sugar from Barbados. Its south front is embellished by the sundial made by Wren and removed from the south wall of the chapel. The telescopic twin towers have been derided as ridiculous and anachronistic,

[1] His designs have been reproduced by the Clarendon Press (1959), and can be acquired from the College.

but no lover of Oxford would be without them. The Fellows' common room is on the ground floor between them and its windows look out across the grass to the wrought-iron gate under the cupola of the cloister screen and the superb dome of the Radcliffe Camera towering above it.

In the course of years the Wardens gradually moved eastwards from the gate-tower until they came to a stop in the beautiful Queen Anne house designed by Dr. Clarke and built in 1704–6.

Famous men: Thomas Linacre; Robert Recorde; Gilbert Sheldon, Archbishop of Canterbury; Jeremy Taylor (from Cambridge); Thomas Sydenham; Sir Christopher Wren; Sir William Blackstone; Robert Cecil, third Marquess of Salisbury; Sir W. R. Anson; George Nathaniel, Marquess Curzon of Kedleston; Hensley Henson, Bishop of Durham; Cosmo Gordon Lang, Archbishop of Canterbury; T. E. Lawrence; Sir John, first Viscount Simon; Lionel Curtis; Edward Wood, first Earl of Halifax; Leopold Amery; Sir Sarvapalli Radhakrishnan, President of India.

On coming out of All Souls and turning right we may go along Catte Street and visit Hertford and New College or we may first look at the University Church, Brasenose College, and the Radcliffe Camera. We will do the latter.

From its earliest days the University has used the Church of ST. MARY THE VIRGIN. It was used for meetings of Congregation, for disputations, degree ceremonies, trials, but it is not known how the University came to appropriate it. Except for the Cathedral it is the largest church in Oxford. Its most striking features, the tower, *c.* 1280, and the spire, *c.* 1320, are its oldest, though these were repaired twice in the nineteenth century and with one exception the giant statues are modern copies of the originals, some of which will be found in the old Congregation House adjoining and four of which are in New College cloister.

The south porch, with its twisted pillars, curved pediment, and angels that have now lost their heads, is a rare example of English baroque and another instance of how well contrasting architectural styles will blend so long as they are good in themselves and on the right scale. It was the gift of Dr. Morgan Owen, Bishop of Llandaff, Chancellor of the University, and friend of Laud, 1637.

The nave and chancel were rebuilt in the fifteenth cen-

15. Brasenose College: hall

16. The Radcliffe Camera

17. Hertford College
with New College tower
and chapel beyond

18. New College:
garden gate with
city wall beyond

tury, 1463–90, but Adam de Brome's chapel on the north side dates from 1328. He was rector of the church and Founder of Oriel College, which still appoints the vicar.

Galleries were erected in 1827, but have now been removed except for that at the west end, which is used by undergraduates attending University Sermons. The seats of the Vice-Chancellor and Proctors are also at the west end.

In the chancel the cedar communion rails of 1673 and the fifteenth-century stalls, sedilia, and reredos are worthy of note. The organ built by Bernard Schmidt in 1674 was burnt out in 1947.

The church has been the scene of many stirring events, the most famous being the humiliation of the city after the battle of St. Scholastica's Day in 1355; the moving and terrible trials of the heroic bishops, Latimer, Ridley, and Cranmer (all Cambridge men) in 1555–6; sermons by Wesley, Keble, and Newman, the first starting the Methodist revival and the latter two the Oxford Movement which, by action and reaction, revitalized and transformed the Church of England.

There are six heavy bells, all seventeenth-century, and these are pealed or tolled on University occasions, e.g. at the admission of the Vice-Chancellor in October and of the Proctors in March, at Encaenia, and always for half an hour before meetings of Congregation and Convocation. The University Sermon is preached here on most Sundays in term at 10.15 a.m. In alternate years eight of these in the Hilary and Trinity Terms constitute the famous lectures founded by the Rev. John Bampton in 1751. From 1954–5 these lectures have been supplemented in the other years by the Sarum Lectures, paid for out of the surplus of the same endowment.

If we leave the church by the north door and turn right we shall see a building separate from the church and standing in the angle made by the tower and the chancel. This is the first building which the University possessed and was the gift of Thomas Cobham, Bishop of Worcester, in 1320. The vaulted chamber in the ground floor was the Congregation House and the room above was the first University library. Now the lower room is used as a chapel and houses crumbling effigies removed from the spire. The upper room is used for parish meetings. In the fifteenth century the north windows were altered to give the outside the appearance of a one-storied building to match the church.

On the west side of Radcliffe Square and facing All Souls is

BRASENOSE COLLEGE

Founded 1509. *Present strength*: The Principal; 37 Fellows; 17 lecturers; 11 senior scholars; 43 scholars; 77 exhibitioners; 264 other members receiving tuition or supervision. *Buildings*: gatehouse, 1509; chapel, 1656–66; hall, 1509; library 1664; Old quadrangle, 1509–16; third quadrangle, 1880–1909; kitchen, fifteenth-century; new building, 1959–61.

 BRASENOSE, often called 'B.N.C.', but whose full title is 'the King's Hall and College of Brasenose', takes its name from the form of the door-knocker of the hall which had occupied the site at the corner of Schools Street and St. Mildred's Lane from the thirteenth century and which, by the munificence of William Smyth, Bishop of Lincoln (d. 1514), and Sir Richard Sutton, a lawyer (d. 1524), who both came from the same district of Prescot and Presbury, in Lancashire, became a College in 1509. The last Principal of the Hall was the first Principal of the College.

The early history of the College was not without some sordid financial scandals and corruption which more than once brought it to the verge of bankruptcy. A great evil was the relative wealth of the Principal and six Senior Fellows and the poverty of the Juniors. Thus in 1588 the Seniors had £200 p.a. and the Juniors only £40, with the consequence that many of the latter became embittered and went out of residence. Yet, despite these handicaps and the factions they engendered, the College attracted substantial scholarship endowments, notably the Hulme and Somerset benefactions which strengthened the ties of the College with Lancashire in the late seventeenth century.

The Founders' statutes had permitted the admission of

six sons of noblemen at their own expense and the number of commoners and gentlemen commoners greatly increased until there were twenty-eight scholars, thirty-five graduates, and eighty-seven undergraduates in 1612. But we are told that in the eighteenth century 'the privileges of the gentlemen commoners were already being undermined. They lost many valued rights, such as hiring cock-lofts for their servants, dining at the high table, and being made members of the common-room. They were made to do the same exercises as other undergraduates. The tutorial system, even in bad periods, ensured a minimum standard of ability and industry. In 1670 Mr. Edward Moore was advised to remove his brother: "His intellectuals are not for these studies . . . as for his morals, if a strict eye be kept over them, I hope they may be good." John Kenrick in 1750 describes his entrance examination and states that the system of college teaching makes "our confinement here as great as at school. . . . With our private tutor we are lectured upon Plato's Dialogues and Logic, whenever he pleases to call upon us; for our public lectures in the hall, we have particular days in the week, which consists of Xenophon's *Memorabilia* and Horace, by two different lecturers, one of whom is Mr. Mather, a very ingenious man, whom I daresay you have heard of. As for our exercises, they are disputations, three times a week, besides a Declamation every term".[1]

Brasenose has usually enjoyed a pre-eminent reputation on the games field and on the river, but she rarely lacked distinction in the Schools.

The nucleus of the site of B.N.C. was part of the property bought by the University in 1262 with money out of William of Durham's bequest (see p. 6) and it was from University College that the Founders acquired the freehold in 1509. Of Brasenose Hall the only building remaining is the kitchen. The gate-tower, which was the Principal's Lodging, is one of the finest in Oxford, and must have looked even better before the flanking roofs were raised, a new story being added in 1605–36. The tendency to add a story to old college

[1] *V.C.H. Oxfordshire*, iii. 211–12.

buildings—and even to new ones—has destroyed the proportions of a good many things both in Oxford and Cambridge.

The hall is a charming piece of sixteenth-century work outside and of eighteenth-century comfort and elegance inside. In 1748 the fire-place superseded the charcoal brazier, from which the fumes had escaped through the central louvre; the present plaster ceiling was constructed in 1754. There are some good portraits. The Brazen Nose above the High Table was recovered in 1890 from Stamford, to which place there had been a migration of Oxford students in 1333, but the Nose still on the front gate has been there since the days of the hall.

The old chapel was on the first floor to the west of the hall and the old library was in a corresponding position in the north range opposite. After the new chapel was built the old one became the Senior Common Room and the old library was turned into rooms.

As with Queen's, so with B.N.C., the only way to expand was towards the High Street. The original quadrangle stood on the site of seven halls, Brasenose, Ivy Hall, University Hall, Sheld Hall, St. Thomas Hall, Salysurry, and St. Mary's Entry. In the seventeenth century the College absorbed on its south side Little Edmund Hall and Haberdasher Hall and also took in Black Hall and Glass Hall on the other side of School Street (all that side of the street disappeared when the Camera was built). This extension enabled the present chapel to be begun in 1656. The bulk of the money for it came from a bequest of Principal Samuel Radcliffe and it took ten years to build. The library, finished in 1664, was brilliantly restored and enlarged in 1960. Both are an odd mixture of the Gothic and classical styles, a fact partly accounted for by the use of old material from Little Edmund Hall and from St. Mary's College, which until the Dissolution was the College of the Augustinian Canons in New Inn Hall Street. B.N.C. acquired this property, with Frewin Hall, which she still possesses, in 1580. The fine hammer-beam roof of St. Mary's Chapel became the roof of B.N.C.'s chapel and was then, alas, concealed in elaborate 'fan-vaulting' made of plaster (1659). The chapel stalls are of the same period and the lectern and chandeliers are eighteenth-century.

The third quadrangle, long projected, was finally designed by Sir T. G. Jackson, R.A., and completed in 1886–1909. The College deserves credit for having resisted the temptation to allow shops on the ground floor facing the streets, though the rents would have been a valuable source of revenue.

There was not much room on the Brasenose site for further building, but to meet the pressures of the 1960's new sets of rooms for twenty-five undergraduates were built west of Jackson's quadrangle in 1959–61, and bicycles and baths were put underground: the architects were Powell and Moya.

Famous men: Alexander Nowell; John Foxe; Lord Ellesmere (Lord Chancellor); Robert Burton; William Petty; Thomas Traherne; Henry Addington (Viscount Sidmouth); Walter Pater; Earl Haig; John Buchan; Charles Morgan; John Middleton Murry.

THE RADCLIFFE LIBRARY or CAMERA is as grand and perfect a building as any in Oxford and it speaks for itself in the language of the eighteenth century with no less emphasis than the spire of St. Mary's in the accents of the fourteenth: the one typical of the Age of Reason, the other of the Age of Faith. Yet they are admirable neighbours, both in their relation to each other and to the colleges around them.

Dr. John Radcliffe was not a man to be deterred by difficulties. In his will he left £40,000 for the erection of a library which was eventually built on a site already cluttered with buildings, the area between St. Mary's and the old Schools. It took more than twenty years of negotiations to clear the ground and building began in May 1737. It was finished in 1748 and opened in 1749 when the Vice-Chancellor, Dr. William King, Principal of St. Mary Hall, took the occasion to deliver a violent Jacobite speech. Not till 1760 did Oxford find it possible to be loyal to the House of Hanover.

James Gibbs was the architect[1] and it is said to be the earliest example in England of a round library. But Wren, in 1675, had first proposed a round one for Trinity College, Cambridge, albeit it was to have risen from a square plinth.

The Camera was originally intended as a science library, but it has for many years now served as a general reading-room of the Bodleian; the Science Library is now by the Museum in Parks Road. A tunnel containing a conveyor-belt system for the efficient delivery of books connects the Camera with the Bodleian. Iron railings encircled the grass from 1827 till 1936 when Lord Greene paid for their removal.

The next college in Catte Street, lying to the north of All Souls and opposite the Schools tower is

HERTFORD COLLEGE

Founded 1874. *Present strength*: The Principal; 22 Fellows; 9 lecturers; 60 scholars; 39 exhibitioners; 2 bible clerks; 210 B.A.s and commoners. *Buildings*: gatehouse, 1887; chapel, 1908; hall, 1889; library, 1716; first quadrangle, *c.* 1600–1889; second quadrangle, 1903–31.

 THE earliest extant document mentioning Hart Hall by name is dated 1301, and refers to a tenement bought by Elias de Hertford in 1283. In 1312 Hart Hall passed into the hands of Walter de Stapeldon, Bishop of Exeter, who was about to found Exeter College, and for several centuries Exeter, as landlord, leased the Hall to a series of Principals who paid their rent and ran it for their own profit. William of Wykeham leased the Hall for his young men while they were waiting to enter into possession of New College, which they did in 1386, and then the link with Exeter was resumed, though under the long reign of Philip Randell, 1549–88, the connexion grew weak again. Since the Hall was only one of eight or ten

[1] He also built St. Mary le Strand, St. Martin-in-the-Fields, and the Gibbs Building at King's College, Cambridge.

occupying the restricted site of the present College it had not much scope until these weakened and failed and their properties could be gradually absorbed.

It was in the eighteenth century that Hart Hall first became a College under the Principalship of the eccentric, enthusiastic, 'crack-brained' Dr. Richard Newton. He embodied his educational theories in a new set of statutes and planned in detail the education of the College complement of thirty-two undergraduates, eight of whom were to be admitted each year for a four-year course. His careful programme and strict discipline made him popular with parents and the College was full. Unfortunately his application for a charter of incorporation as a College was opposed by Exeter and he did not get it till 1740, fourteen years after the benefactor who had promised him the indispensable endowment had died. Newton himself died in 1753 and the poverty-stricken College soon declined. After 1805 no one could be found to take over the Principalship, though Vice-Principal Hewitt, the only don left, carried on till 1818.

Meanwhile Magdalen had, for more than 100 years, been anxious to extrude its inconvenient neighbour, Magdalen Hall, a society which had flourished particularly in the seventeenth century and which had existed on what is now the site of St. Swithun's quadrangle (p. 45) since *c.* 1487. Wise men put their heads together and a scheme was devised whereby Hertford's property escheated to the Crown, which then regranted it to the University in trust for Magdalen Hall. A small sum was kept back to provide a pension for the pathetic Hewitt and when he died the income was used for the Hertford scholarship, worth about £60, which is awarded every year after an examination in Latin. In 1820 matters were hastened by the burning down of Magdalen Hall after an undergraduate party and in 1822 its members moved into enlarged buildings on the Hertford site.

Magdalen Hall had some valuable scholarships and had built up a good reputation, sufficient to induce Mr. T. C. Baring of the great banking house, a former exhibitioner of Wadham and Fellow of Brasenose College, to give a substantial benefaction for Fellowships and scholarships, enough to turn it into a College once more. The name of Hertford was resumed and the charter of incorporation was dated 1874. From 1877 till 1922 the College had the good fortune to be ruled by a great and lovable man, the Rev. Henry Boyd, D.D., who set it firmly on its feet.

The buildings are not distinguished, but they are pleasant and offer a wide range of styles. The two wings of the front were built for Magdalen Hall in 1820–2 (architect, E. W. Garbett) and these were joined by the hall over the gate in 1887. Sir T. G. Jackson, R.A., was the architect for this and for the 'Bridge of Sighs' over New College Lane and the North quadrangle (1903–31) in which was incorporated the ancient octagonal chapel of Our Lady at Smith Gate, 1931.

The oldest part of the main quadrangle is the north-east corner, a block built by Philip Randell c. 1560: it included the old hall and buttery; the third story was added c. 1700. The east range was built by Dr. Philip Price, Principal 1604–31. The eighteenth-century chapel is now the library and the present chapel, one of Sir T. G. Jackson's most successful buildings, was finished in 1908.

The doors which hang at the main entrance were made at the end of the seventeenth century for a 'monumental gateway in Catte Street'[1] built by Principal Thornton (1688–1707).

Famous men: *Hart Hall*: John Donne, poet and Dean of St. Paul's; John Selden; Lord Henry Pelham, Prime Minister; and Charles James Fox; *Magdalen Hall*: William Tyndale; Thomas Hobbes; John Wilkins; Sir Henry Vane; Sir Matthew Hale; Edward Hyde, Earl of Clarendon; and *Hertford College*: W. R. Inge, Dean of St. Paul's (Fellow); Lord Quickswood, formerly Lord Hugh Cecil (Fellow).

Before we turn the corner into New College Lane, we should look back at that unrivalled architectural vista (which Thomas Sharp has pointed out) of cube, cylinder, cone— the old Schools, Camera, and St. Mary's.

As we go down New College Lane, we may note how well the fourteenth-century hard stone of cloister and barn has worn. It came from the Wheatley quarries before the best seams were exhausted.[2]

[1] *V.C.H. Oxfordshire*, iii. 312.   [2] W. J. Arkell, *Oxford Stone*, p. 39.

19. Wadham College: the garden

20. Clarendon Building

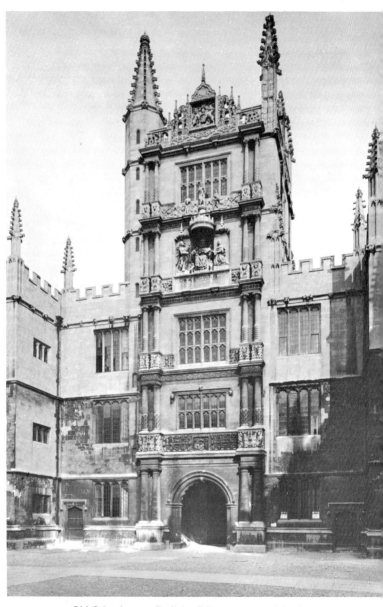

21. Old Schools, now Bodleian Library: tower of the Five Orders

NEW COLLEGE

Founded 1379. *Present strength*: The Warden; 42 Fellows; 4 Research Fellows;
13 lecturers; 11 senior scholars; 70 scholars; 42 exhibitioners; 4 clerks and
20 choristers; 292 B.A.s and commoners. *Buildings*: gatehouse, 1380; chapel,
hall, library, first quadrangle, 1380–6; third storey, 1675; Garden quadrangle, 1682–1711; cloister and bell-tower, 1400; city walls, thirteenth and
fourteenth centuries; Holywell Buildings, 1872–96; Memorial Library,
1939; Sacher Building, 1962.

 MORE than with any other Oxford founda-
tion, the history of New College is the history
of its buildings. They began as a magnificent
conception, far exceeding any educational
experiment which had gone before and the
wealth and generosity of the founder, William
of Wykeham, were such that nothing was left
undone that could be done.

He was a wealthy pluralist, canon or prebendary of
fifteen churches, Surveyor of the King's Castles, Bishop of
Winchester 1367–1404, and twice Lord High Chancellor
of England. A great figure in the reigns of Edward III and
Richard II, he was much concerned with the way plague
and disease—the ravages of the Black Death began in 1348—
had reduced the number of clergy and, as we should call it,
the civil service, and he wanted to ensure for the future
a steady supply of well-educated men for the service of
Church and State. Having himself been educated at Winchester, he decided to found a school there which should
give a good grounding in grammar to boys who might at
about sixteen years old pass on to another college built
exclusively for them at Oxford. At twenty-two or twenty-
three they would incept as Masters of Arts and either then
go out into the Church or remain to teach or take higher
degrees in Theology, Law, or Medicine. Of course all took
Holy Orders at an early stage in their Oxford career.

It was in order to distinguish it from the other 'House
of the Blessed Virgin in Oxford, commonly called Oriel
College', that Wykeham's foundation, officially called 'St.
Mary College of Winchester in Oxford', has always been
known as New College.

The Bishop was lucky to find a large site vacant, possibly

as the result of plague, inside the north-east corner of the city walls. He had to undertake to keep the walls in repair and to give access to the Mayor to view them every third year. The quadrangle was begun in 1380 and finished in 1386. New College Lane had to be diverted to make room for the cloister, which was consecrated in 1400, when the bell-tower was also completed. The figures on both sides of the gate-tower are of the Virgin, St. Gabriel, and the Founder. The oak doors are original and date from the fourteenth century.

The quadrangle was the first in Oxford and set the fashion for the future (the earliest surviving college quadrangle is the Old Court at Corpus Christi College, Cambridge, 1348, but that was on a much smaller scale). Its north side is taken up with the lofty line of chapel and hall. Over the hall stairs rises the Muniment Tower and carried over the arch on the east side is the Founder's Library. On the south and part of the west sides are Fellows' chambers: each set consisted of one large room to sleep in and three or four studies. The gate-house and neighbouring rooms provided quarters for the Warden and the porter. Unfortunately an extra story was added on three sides in 1675 and their architectural relationship to the towers and chapel spoiled.

The kitchen, buttery, larders, beer-cellar, servants' and cook's quarters were out of sight and sound, eastwards of the hall, and the Long Room, consisting of latrines upstairs and a vast cess-pool on the ground floor, was outside the south-east corner of the quad, along Queen's Lane.[1] Supplies for the kitchen came through the *non licet* gate in Queen's Lane and never disturbed the quiet of chapel and chambers. The garden provided fruit and vegetables.

If on entering the quadrangle we turn left we shall find in the corner a passage leading to chapel and cloister. The

[1] Robert Plot, first Curator of the Ashmolean Museum, after writing of the vaulting of the Divinity School and the hall stairs at Christ Church says: 'And were it not improper amongst these to mention a structure of so inferior a quality, as *New College* house of *Easement*, commonly called the *long house*, I could not but note it as a stupendous piece of building, it being so large and deep, that it has never been emptied since the foundation of the *College*, which was above 300 years since, nor is ever likely to want it.' *The Natural History of Oxfordshire* (Oxford, 1677).

cloister is exceptional in that it was built entirely for its own sake and is not backed, as is commonly the case, by other buildings to which it is incidental, as at most monasteries or at Magdalen and Christ Church. It was for processions and exercise and it enclosed a burial ground. Despite the clock in the great bell-tower beside it, it has an air of peace and timelessness. The tower supplanted a bastion on the city wall and its first clock lasted from *c.* 1455 till 1655, when it had to be replaced. The present clock was installed in 1884. There are ten bells, all dated between 1655 and 1723.

Returning from the cloister, we find the door to the ante-chapel on our left. The ante-chapel is really a short nave of two bays and its purpose was to provide room for side altars, of which there were originally six, and a place for disputations. The glass, except for the great west window, is fourteenth-century. It was removed during the Second World War and replaced at enormous expense. The west window, now fading, is from cartoons of Sir Joshua Reynolds, 1778–85; its medieval glass, sold for £30, found its way to York Minster where it is still. Below is Epstein's *Lazarus*, not to be lightly dismissed as a piece of eccentric modernity; it is especially striking as one comes down to it from the east end. High up in the south wall can be seen two slits in the stone: they are squints from the Warden's oratory, from which he could hear Mass or disputations without going down to them. The oratory was converted into his study in the seventeenth century. Also on the south wall are the names of those men of New College who fell in the First World War and near them on the east wall are the names of three German members of the College who fell fighting for their country: an unusual tribute. The stalls were formerly a second range erected in the choir in 1638, but were thrown out by Wyatt in 1790.

The choir has undergone many changes since its first perfection. We are told that the figures of the first reredos, destroyed at the Reformation, were *subtiliter fabricata variisque coloribus perornata*.[1] And when Wyatt was dealing with the east wall at the end of the eighteenth century he found

[1] Delicately made and adorned with many colours.

the niches a deep ultramarine blue and the carved work richly gilt. The Reformers removed the organ and there was none till 1597: this in turn was destroyed by the Puritans and yet another had to be installed at the Restoration. The present organ came into use in 1969. Of the original stalls little more than the misericords remains: they merit close inspection. The hammer-beam roof of Sir Gilbert Scott, 1877–81, replaced a plaster vault erected by Wyatt, 1789–94. The present reredos and statues date from 1888–91. The glass in the choir is of the eighteenth century. In the north wall, near the vestry door, will be found in a glass case one of the College's greatest treasures, the Founder's crosier, silver-gilt, richly worked with enamelled panels and set with jewels. Near by is El Greco's exquisite painting of St. James, given to the College by Mr. A. E. Allnatt in 1961. The doors of the screen are fourteenth-century.

The hall is reached up the steps under the Muniment Tower. It is a fine room, but the unlovely coloured glass makes it gloomy. It was glazed from the beginning and before the linen-fold panelling was installed in 1533 the walls were hung with painted cloth. The roof is a modern imitation of the original, by Sir Gilbert Scott, 1865. There are some interesting portraits of the Founder and Archbishop Warham, and of two recent Wardens, H. A. L. Fisher and W. A. Spooner, the alleged inventor of the 'spoonerism'. The Epstein bust is of A. H. Smith, Warden 1944–58.

Stairs down from the screen lead to buttery, kitchen, &c., and a circular stair up, reached through a pair of locked doors, leads to the two upper stages of the Muniment Tower. The rooms, which contain the title-deeds to the College properties, scattered over a dozen counties, and the bursars' records and admission registers going back to the beginning, are guarded by massive iron-bound doors, each with a set of ponderous locks and keys. The ceilings are stone-vaulted, the floors are paved with the original coloured tiles and iron grids defend the narrow windows.

On the ground floor of the tower, next to the stairs, is the Treasury, where the principal treasures of the College may from time to time be seen. They include various relics of the Founder—his mitre, rings, &c.; the Renaissance plate of the College, together with the chapel plate, and the famous 'unicorn's horn'.

The Founder's Library and the Wyatt Room (remodelled in 1778) above it are fine chambers and have recently been restored, the original chestnut flooring being relaid in the first, after beams infected with beetle had been removed.

Going through the arch we come into the Garden quadrangle, the wings of which open out in three successive stages. The first pair was built in 1683–4 and the second pair in 1700–11. A fine wrought-iron railing (1711) divides the court from the garden. This cunning design of the extension had the effect of completely masking the Long Room and the kitchen, which would have been great eyesores for any building erected in the garden and facing westwards to the old quadrangle.

The garden is L-shaped, having been extended in 1500 by the purchase from Magdalen of three plots east of St. Peter's Church. Its most remarkable features are the stretch of city wall restored in the fourteenth century; the mound, a queer piece of landscape gardening, begun in 1594 and completed in 1623; and the views of Magdalen Tower and St. Peter-in-the-East.

Beyond the wall is the Sacher building for 40 graduate students. It is the gift of Mr. Harry Sacher; architect David Roberts (1962). The sculpture on the lawn is by Barbara Hepworth and was acquired in 1964.

If we go out of the garden through an arch in the city wall (which had to be made in 1700 when access to the kitchen via the *non licet* gate was made impossible by the building of the garden court), we see not only the outside of the city wall, but also the vast range of buildings erected by Gilbert Scott in 1872 and extended eastwards by Basil Champneys in 1885 and 1896. It is the latter's Robinson Tower which joins his lower building to Scott's and it is only fair to Scott to say that the College spoilt the scale of his building by insisting on an extra storey, thus shutting the sun out of Holywell Street and destroying the view from the north.

The Memorial Library at the west end of this plot was

built in the Egyptian style by Sir Hubert Worthington and completed in 1939.

The College was founded for a Warden, seventy Fellows and scholars, ten chaplains, three clerks, and sixteen choristers, and, unlike previous colleges and many halls, it was specifically intended for undergraduates who should be prepared by their seniors for their degrees in arts: possibly the first instance of the 'tutorial system'. All were to come up from Winchester College and must be between fifteen and twenty years of age. They must not possess an annual income of more than £3. 6s. 8d. and must swear to remain for at least five years, the two first as probationers, after which they were full Fellows. The Warden had to be a New College man in priest's Orders over thirty years of age. He had £40 a year and an entertainment allowance as well as travelling expenses when engaged on College business. Six horses were provided for him and it was his duty, with a Fellow and a bursary clerk, to ride round the College estates each September. He dined in hall only on gaudy days and was allowed two months' leave annually.

There were strict rules about attendance at chapel, residence (vacations were short, the longest being from 16 August till 1 October), and rowdy games: it was not allowed to play ball in chapel. Latin was always to be spoken. There was a full domestic staff and plenty of good food, even on fast days, and every Fellow received an annual issue of cloth for livery.

New College led the way with the New Learning. It was Warden Chandler, 1454–75, who brought Vitelli to Oxford to give the first Greek lectures that Oxford heard. William Grocyn was a Fellow from 1465 till 1480. But the religious troubles of the Reformation introduced a period of laxity and corruption. Corrupt resignations became as much an evil at New College as they were at All Souls and there was a scandalous influx of Founder's kin. At the time of the Commonwealth the Warden and over forty Fellows and scholars were expelled and in 1660 nineteen. After that the College gradually sank to its lowest ebb. That it was rich and that it was recruited from one only source, Winchester,

76

were great evils, but a worse was that its members never had to take University tests for their degrees. These had always been granted on the word of the Warden that candidates were fit. This privilege was not resigned till 1834 and during the next twenty years the College got only one First in the Schools. But from the time of the University Commission when a proportion of the Fellowships and scholarships were thrown open the College proceeded to take a leading place in the University intellectually, socially, and in every other way.

Famous men: Henry Chichele, Archbishop of Canterbury; John Russell, Bishop of Lincoln and Lord Chancellor; William Grocyn; William Warham, Archbishop of Canterbury; Sir Henry Wotton; Thomas Ken, Bishop of Bath and Wells; Francis Turner, Bishop of Ely; Robert Lowth, Bishop of London; William Howley, Archbishop of Canterbury; Sydney Smith; John Galsworthy, O.M.; H. A. L. Fisher, O.M.; Sir Maurice Bowra, C.H.; Sir A. P. Herbert; George Woodcock.

We may leave New College either by the way we came in (regaining the front quadrangle by going through another arch in the city wall and under the hall by a vaulted passage, 1872) or, if the north gate is open, we may go out into Holywell Street. One side of this is still lined with delightful old houses of the seventeenth and eighteenth centuries, and their occupants have had the imagination to paint them in various colours. If we turn left we shall soon see, on our right, the Music Room, 1742, and the buildings of the Faculty of Music. The Music Room is the oldest in Europe and was known to Handel. It stands on Wadham ground and is leased to the University. Music, especially for ecclesiastical purposes, formed a part of the University curriculum from the beginning. The Heather Professorship of Music dates from 1626.

At the end of the street, on our left, is the former Indian Institute, an ugly building of yellow stone, built in the fashion of the time, 1884-96, by Basil Champneys. Its contents have been moved, the books to the penthouse on the roof of the New Bodleian and the ceramics and bronzes to the Ashmolean.

Turning to the right down Parks Road, leaving the Bodleian New Library on our left, and noting the ancient

'King's Arms' hotel, the upper floors of which are now incorporated into Wadham College, on our right, we come to

WADHAM COLLEGE

Founded 1610. *Present strength*: The Warden; 37 Fellows; a chaplain; 15 lecturers; 8 senior scholars; 103 scholars; 265 other members receiving tuition or supervision. *Buildings*: first quadrangle with chapel and library, 1610–13; staircase IX, 1693; New Building, 1951–2; Holywell houses, seventeenth or eighteenth centuries.

 WADHAM is virtually the youngest of the old foundations, for Pembroke, Worcester, and Hertford all had their origins in medieval halls. It was founded 'to the praise, glory and honour of Almighty God, for the increase of sound letters and the common utility of this Kingdom', by Nicholas Wadham, of Merifield in the County of Somerset, Esquire, and Dorothy his wife, daughter of Sir William Petre. Both were of distinguished ancestry and they had large estates and no children. At the end of his life Wadham decided to devote part of his personal fortune, amounting to about £19,200, to the foundation of a college at Oxford. He died in October 1609 and his widow carried out his intentions, adding a further endowment from her own resources of about £7,300.

The vacant site of the great Augustinian friary, outside Smith Gate, at the corner of Holywell, was bought from the city for £600, though they had asked £1,000 for it. Craftsmen in wood and stone were brought up from Somerset, Magdalen permitted the use of quarries at Headington, and building began in April 1610. It was finished in July 1613.

The buildings are remarkable for the simplicity, and the symmetry of their design; they have never had to be substantially altered and they stand now as they did 350 years ago. The designer and builder was a well-known west-country architect, William Arnold, who had probably built Montacute House and had certainly carried out important work at Dunster Castle and Cranborne House. The style

22. Bodleian Library: Arts End

23. Divinity School

24. Convocation House

adopted was a mixture of Gothic and Jacobean, the former being used for the chapel windows and the latter for the frontispiece between hall and ante-chapel and the hall and chapel screens.

The front of the College, which originally lay behind a small walled forecourt, gives the impression of being low and long despite its three stories. The gate-tower in the middle with its oriel is balanced by the gables at each end and the great bay windows below them. A daring feature is the four lofty chimney-stacks, flush with the walls, like stakes to pin the College down.

The quadrangle (134 ft. × 122 ft.) is relatively large and is exceeded only by those at Christ Church, Magdalen, and New College, among those that are older.

The figures over the hall stairs are of James I and the founders, with the royal arms above (originally Stuart but now Hanoverian). The hall is one of the finest in Oxford and ranks third for size after those of Christ Church and New College. Noteworthy features are the hammer-beam roof and the Jacobean screen. The fire-place was inserted in 1826; before that a brazier stood in the middle of the floor, which was then paved with stone. The coats of arms in the south window commemorate benefactors and in the great bay window, distinguished sons of the College. Some are the work of Thomas Willement in 1827 and the rest date from 1897.

The stone-vaulted kitchen, with library above it, runs eastwards from the hall and at right angles to it, and these balance the chapel.

The west door of the chapel is in the quadrangle, but the usual entrance for visitors is in the passage leading to the garden. Both ante-chapel and chapel are finely proportioned and unusually large. The east window by Bernard van Linge is dated 1622 and is brilliantly successful. The Jacobean communion table came in 1889 from Ilminster Church, where the Wadhams are buried, but the tabernacle work, introduced by Blore in 1832–4, is of a hard and alien stone quite out of keeping with the rest of the place. It was he who also substituted the ugly stucco ceiling for one of boards 'divided into panels with rosettes at the intersections'. The Jacobean stalls and screen are good, and have the unusual feature of servants' pews, erected behind the screen. The cedar altar-rails, of about 1670, are comparable with those at Oriel, Lincoln, and Trinity. The lectern was given by Sir Thomas Lear, Bt., in 1691.

The garden is famed for the view it gives of the north front of the College and for its cedar and copper-beech trees, while, in season, the herbaceous border is second to none in Oxford. The Warden's garden adjoins it on the west and north. In 1926 two acres were sold to the Rhodes Trustees for the erection of Rhodes House.

The Holywell quadrangle lies to the south and takes in all the houses along the street. No. 9 staircase dates from 1693; Nos. 10 and 11 are later, but the great feature is the New Building erected in 1948–53 to the designs of H. G. Goddard. It is roughly L -shaped and includes a Junior Common Room and bar with library above and twenty-three sets of rooms for undergraduates. Beyond it is a unique undergraduates' garden. The whole conception is good, executed in the right materials and on the right scale.

Plans are in being for a large extension on the east between the buildings of the Music Faculty and Savile Road. This is to include a new library to the cost of which the Iranian Imperial Foundation has contributed £125,000, and it is hoped that this will stimulate new interest in Persian studies. The library will bear the name of the Shah's twin sister, Princess Ashraf Pahlavi. The architects are Gillespie, Kidd and Coia, of Glasgow.

The College began with a Warden, fifteen Fellows, fifteen scholars, two chaplains, two bible-clerks, and twenty-seven gentlemen commoners and battellars. The statutes were unusual in requiring the Warden to be unmarried (a provision only repealed in 1806), in allowing Fellows to be laymen, and in limiting the tenure of Fellowships to eighteen years. Most of its members came from Somerset, Devon, and Cornwall.

Throughout its history the College tended to be 'Whig' and 'Low Church' and in 1618 it successfully resisted an attempt by James I to foist a Scotsman into a Fellowship when he was by statute ineligible. The very next year the College Register recorded great satisfaction on the admission as Fellow-commoner of Carew Ralegh, son of the great Sir Walter, whom James had just executed. During the Civil War the King seized all the College's silver, except the chapel plate; there was 123 lb. of it.

At the conclusion of the war, in 1648, the Warden and three-quarters of the College were ejected, but a great period in Wadham's history began with the appointment of John Wilkins as Warden in that year. He married Cromwell's sister in 1656 and after a brief period as Master of Trinity College, Cambridge, became Bishop of Chester. It was in his lodgings and under his leadership that there assembled a group who formed the Oxford nucleus of what was later to become the Royal Society. Christopher Wren, matriculated 1649, together with Seth Ward and Lawrence Rooke, both from Cambridge, and Thomas Sprat, matriculated 1651, were Wadham members of that famous body. In 1688 it was Gilbert Ironside, Warden, who as Vice-Chancellor resisted James II's attempt to impose Romanism on Magdalen and the University and another Wadham man, John, Lord Lovelace, was prominent in his support of William III.

During the eighteenth century Wadham went into serious decline in numbers and reputation, but her academic record was outstanding in the first decades of the nineteenth century. She was then markedly evangelical, though R. W. Church was matriculated in 1832. The Positivists or 'Comtists' also found a home there under the leadership of Richard Congreve, Frederic Harrison, and E. S. Beesley. A recent great burst of Wadham brilliance was in the early nineties when C. B. Fry, F. E. Smith, J. A. Simon, A. A. Roche, F. W. Hirst, and C. R. Hone were at the scholars' table together and in the same Rugby XV.

Famous men: Robert Blake, admiral; Sir Christopher Wren; John Wilkins; John Wilmot, second Earl of Rochester; Sir Charles Sedley, Bt.; Arthur Onslow, Speaker 1726–61; R. W. Church, Dean of St. Paul's; Richard Bethell, Lord Westbury, Lord Chancellor; Frederic Harrison; Sir T. G. Jackson, Bt., R.A.; F. E. Smith, first Earl of Birkenhead, Lord Chancellor;

J. A., first Viscount Simon, Lord Chancellor; C. B. Fry; Sir Thomas Beecham, Bt.; Sir Firoz Khan Noon, Prime Minister of Pakistan; Cecil Day Lewis, Poet Laureate; Sir Maurice Bowra (Warden).

Almost exactly opposite Wadham are the handsome garden gates of Trinity with a lovely view of its Garden quadrangle and the antique gables of its Durham buildings, but we turn back towards Broad Street to the new Bodleian.

The architect, Sir Giles Gilbert Scott, O.M., R.A., was faced with a difficult problem when he had to plan a vast extension to the BODLEIAN LIBRARY on a small rectangle of ground without getting things out of scale and offending neighbouring buildings of great distinction. His brilliant achievement at Oxford may be contrasted with his new University Library at Cambridge where he had virtually unlimited scope and a virgin site.

The New Library is, like so many of the latest Oxford buildings, of Bladon stone with Clipsham dressings. It consists of a central core of eleven floors of book stacks, three of which are underground, capable of holding 5 million volumes. There is also a large reading-room and many other rooms for particular research. The building was finished in 1940 and was formally opened for its proper purpose by King George VI in October 1946. It cost £1 million, of which the Rockefeller Foundation gave three-fifths. An underground tunnel with conveyor belt joins the old and new libraries.

On the opposite corner of Broad Street stands the CLARENDON BUILDING, home of the University Press from 1713 till 1829, when it moved to Walton Street. It was built by Nicholas Hawksmoor and was partly paid for by the profits from the publication in 1702–4 of Clarendon's *History of the Great Rebellion*. Clarendon's statue stands in a niche facing west. The leaden figures on the top of the building representing the nine muses—one missing—are by Sir James Thornhill. The beautiful panelled room in the south-west corner is to this day the meeting-place of the Delegates of the University Press, but the rest of the building is the headquarters of the University administration, with offices for the Registrar and Proctors. The wrought-iron gates lend a touch of great beauty and the whole building with its deep recesses is a poem in light and shade.

Immediately to the south is the square of the old Schools, 1613–24. As we enter the quadrangle from the north we see on our left the Tower of the Five Orders (Doric, Tuscan, Ionic, Corinthian, and Composite), an elaborate, pinnacled affair with a statue of James I under a canopy and at the top, in the complicated parapet, the Stuart arms. The University archives are housed on the fourth floor. In the quadrangle below stands a bronze statue by Hubert le Sueur of William Herbert, third Earl of Pembroke. The whole of the rooms we see are now part of the Bodleian Library, but over the doors we may still read the names of the subjects to which the old lecture rooms or 'Schools' were devoted.

The way into the Library is through the *Proscholium* above which is the *Arts End*, lined with seventeenth-century shelves, galleries, and antique folios. Running west from the middle of the Arts End is 'Duke Humphrey', the earliest part of the library, finished in 1490. The elaborate ceiling has the University arms in the panels and Bodley's at every intersection. Corresponding to the Arts End is the *Selden End*, 1634–7. It bears the name of a lawyer and Parliamentarian who was sometime M.P. for the University and who gave to the Bodleian his unique collection of Oriental manuscripts and 8,000 volumes.

The *Proscholium* is so called because it is the vestibule of the Divinity School (1427–90), over which Duke Humphrey is built. The Divinity School has been described as the most beautiful room in Europe. It is the most perfect example in Oxford of that fifteenth-century Perpendicular Gothic which is not met with on the Continent. The vaulted ceiling, partly paid for by a bequest of Cardinal Beaufort, is unexcelled. The doorway on the north was inserted by Wren in place of a window as an egress for processions into the Sheldonian Theatre in 1669.

In the exhibition cases are many Bodleian treasures, including the only known copy of Shakespeare's *Venus and Adonis*, his first published work, 1593; the only known copy of Tottel's *Miscellany*, 1557, and the first book printed by Caxton in England.

The door at the west end of the Divinity School admits us to the Convocation House, 1634, under the Selden End. It is the University's parliament house—the national Parliament met in it more than once when driven from London by the plague—and its panelling, seating, and Vice-Chancellor's throne are all seventeenth-century. It has no artificial light. At its north end is the Vice-Chancellor's court room or *Apodyterium* where cases affecting members of the University were tried.

As we have seen (p. 63), the first University library was over the first Convocation House at St. Mary's. When Humphrey, Duke of Gloucester, brother of Henry V, and a generous patron of learning, offered to give his collection of manuscripts to the University, it was resolved to accommodate them in a new chamber over the Divinity School, then building. The whole was not finished till 1490, some of the delay being due to the unsettled state of the country during the Wars of the Roses. Then, *c.* 1550, the Reforming Commissioners of Edward VI so far destroyed the library that even the empty shelves were also disposed of. What Sir Thomas Bodley saw in 1598 was an empty room. He decided to devote the remainder of his life and his fortune to the reconstitution of the library and its organization and endowment. He enlisted the aid of his friends and the aid of the wealthy and he had the strong support of Sir Henry Savile, Warden of Merton and Provost of Eton. He arranged with the Stationers' Company, which then controlled the output of books, that they would send the library a free copy of every book printed in England. This subsequently became a statutory obligation and the benefits were extended to five other 'copyright' libraries. A Register of Donors was kept and by 1602, when the Library was opened, there were 2,000 volumes. In 1604 Bodley was knighted and next year, when the catalogue showed 6,000 volumes, James I visited the Library. In 1620 there were 16,000 volumes. Now there are over 2 million, including 50,000 volumes of manuscripts. There are also 8,400 rolls and 15,500 charters.

The collection of Oriental manuscripts is the largest in Europe.

Bodley's rules required that the Library should be open as much as possible, that there should be no artificial light, and that no volume should ever be taken away. Neither Charles I nor Cromwell was allowed to break this rule, but heating was introduced in 1821 and lighting in 1929.

Knowing that expansion would be inevitable Bodley built the Arts End and inspired the building of the Schools quadrangle, which was begun on the day of his funeral in 1613. Now, as we have seen, the whole of that quadrangle is part of 'Bodley'.

There are two more buildings in this uninterrupted University group which extends from the University Church to New Bodley. They are the Sheldonian Theatre and the Old Ashmolean.

THE SHELDONIAN THEATRE arose out of the need for some place more suitable than St. Mary's for the great secular functions of the University and, in particular, for the end-of-the-year ceremonies known formerly as the Act and, for the last 300 years, as Encaenia. This takes place at the end of the summer term and is the chief occasion of honorary graduation and commemoration of benefactors. The nature of many of the University ceremonies and disputations, and in particular the rowdyism which often accompanied them, was felt, in an England still influenced by Puritanism, to be improper in a consecrated building; Gilbert Sheldon, formerly Warden of All Souls and soon to be Archbishop of Canterbury, offered to defray the cost of a new building. Wren, at that time Savilian Professor of Astronomy, produced plans partly inspired by engravings of the open-air Theatre of Marcellus in Rome, a city Wren never visited. The ceiling, the span of which (80 ft. × 70 ft.) was far too great for beams in a single length, is an ingenious piece of engineering which was one of the architectural *tours de force* of its period. The painting which covers it (designed to suggest again an open-air theatre) is by Robert Streeter. It represents a cloth on golden cords pulled back to reveal a sky in which the figure of Truth is surrounded by Geometry, Law, Justice, Music, Drama, Architecture, and Astronomy: there are also cherubs and clouds and a falling figure representing Envy, Hatred, and Malice. The illusion of a classical open-air theatre is to a large extent dispelled by the processional door in the centre of what should be the stage and proscenium. The furnishing is seventeenth-century and its carving excellent. The Theatre will seat up to 1,500 people.

The peculiarity of its structure is partly due to the need to provide, in basement and roof, space for printing and storage by the University Press, which continued there till its removal to the Clarendon Building in 1713 (p. 82). In plan the north half is a semicircle and the south half an equivalent rectangle. In the middle of the fine classical south front are the great doors to admit processions and these are flanked with niches containing statues of Sheldon and James Butler, first Duke of Ormonde, who had succeeded him as Chancellor.

In 1800–1 Wren's charming oval dormers, above the balustrading, were removed, and in 1838 Blore substituted his own un-Wren-like cupola for the slimmer and more elegant original.

The choice of stone for the building seems to have been determined mainly by a growing need for economy as the structure grew. A fine-quality stone, perhaps Windrush, was used for the lower half of the south front including mouldings, pilasters, and capitals, and was well enough preserved to be incorporated almost intact in the reconstruction of 1959–60. The same stone was used for some of the carved detail on the north side of the building and around it. In the upper story, however, the cheaper Headington stone was used even for carved swags and capitals, with disastrous results. None of the work now to be seen above the level of the inscription on the south front is seventeenth-century, though it represents a close approximation to what was then done. On the other three sides the facing as a whole is modern, though seventeenth-century carved detail has been kept where possible.

Sheldonian Theatre

Old Ashmolean, now the Museum
the History of Science

27. Exeter College: hall

28. Lincoln College: chapel

It is an open question as to who the figures are that line the street: whether caesars or philosophers, they are hardly human. They were restored in 1868 and again in 1971.

THE OLD ASHMOLEAN MUSEUM stands next door, to the west. It is a perfect piece of English Renaissance work, without parallel in Oxford or Cambridge. The east doorway is incomparably beautiful and on the north side the steps across the area to the first floor and down to the basement, which were removed in 1733, have been restored, in 1958, by the munificence of Mr. J. A. Billmeir.

The building was designed first for the purpose of housing the 'natural curiosities' inherited by Elias Ashmole from John Tradescant and his father, who were great collectors earlier in the seventeenth century, and, secondly, to provide a Natural History School and chemistry laboratory, the first in England. It was finished and opened in 1683 by James, Duke of York, brother of Charles II, whose cipher and crown appear on the north front, and the first Curator and lecturer was Dr. Robert Plot, author of *The Natural History of Oxfordshire*. The architect is not certainly known but was probably a local man, Thomas Wood.

After the building of the Randolph Galleries and New Ashmolean in Beaumont Street (p. 109) it was denuded of its collections and turned to other uses. Within its walls much of the *Oxford English Dictionary* was compiled. As a result of the initiative and energy of Dr. R. T. Gunther the building has since 1935 resumed its former association as the Museum of the History of Science. The basis of the collection was presented by Dr. Lewis Evans in 1925. It contains the best and largest assembly of astrolabes in existence as well as early mathematical instruments. There are also watches and clocks, telescopes and microscopes, surgical instruments, early electric and photographic apparatus and, indeed, examples and illustrations of the history of science, including the discovery of penicillin, for the last 400 years. There is also a valuable specialist library.

We may now either cross Broad Street (formerly Candyche or Horsemonger Street, running east and west outside the city wall) to Trinity and Balliol Colleges or we can turn left down Turl Street. Turl Street derives its name from a revolving or twirling gate that used to be at this end of it.

On our left is

EXETER COLLEGE

Founded 1314. *Present strength*: The Rector; 31 Fellows; 12 lecturers; 45 scholars; 47 exhibitioners; 8 students; 227 members receiving tuition or supervision. *Buildings*: gatehouse, 1701, redesigned 1833; chapel, 1859; hall, 1618; library, 1857; first quadrangle, seventeenth- to eighteenth-century; Palmer's Tower, 1432 (original gatehouse); Broad Street front, 1833–55; Margary quadrangle, 1965.

THREE colleges in Oxford have, so to speak, turned on their axes. Magdalen's main entrance used to face west; Queen's gateway used to look east, and Exeter's looked north, into the little Somnour's Lane, that crept along just inside the city wall and parts of which survive now in St. Michael's Street, Ship Street, and the first part of New College Lane. But whereas Magdalen's fifteenth-century buildings stand as they did, the fourteenth-century quadrangle of Queen's has vanished, and of Exeter's only the former gate-house, Palmer's Tower, remains. We see it standing beyond the chapel, modest but dignified, and shaming by contrast the grandiosity of Scott's pretentious structure.

The present gate-tower began in 1701 as a Palladian successor to the sixteenth-century tower we see in Loggan's print (1675), but its personality was destroyed by a Goth (not to say a Vandal) in 1833 when the whole of the seventeenth- to eighteenth-century front was altered to its present insipid form.

The best thing about Exeter is the hall, built by Sir John Acland in 1618. It has a fine collar-beam roof of Spanish chestnut and a rich Jacobean screen crowned with the Acland arms. The louvre was removed and the fire-places inserted in 1820.

The chambers adjoining the east end of the hall were built at the same time by John Peryam. The rest of the east range succeeded older buildings, including the first library, in 1708.

Meanwhile, in 1623, George Hakewill, who succeeded the great Prideaux as Rector in 1642, had built the only college chapel which had both nave and aisle. The windows resembled those of Wadham (1613) but were larger. They and the richly ornate Jacobean stalls, pulpit, and screen can now be relished only in old prints,[1] for in 1856 this lovely building, which was found to be too small, gave place to Gilbert Scott's imitation of the French Gothic. There are a few old memorials, a fine lectern (1637), and a William Morris tapestry, after the picture, *The Star of Bethlehem*, by Sir Edward Burne-Jones.

The first chapel, 1326, which Hakewill's superseded, was where the present library now stands and it served as the library from 1624 until it was destroyed by fire, with most of the college manuscripts, in 1709. The present library is Scott's work and dates from 1856. It may be seen from the garden, reached by a passage in the south-east corner of the quadrangle. The garden also affords a splendid view of the Divinity School and Bodleian Library.

The Rector's Lodging (altered at the end of the Second World War) is by Scott, who also built most of the north quadrangle facing Broad Street, 1854–5, but that part of it which stands east of the tower was built by Underwood in 1833–4.

Many think that the newest building on the corner of Turl Street and Broad Street continues Exeter's dismal architectural record. It was designed by Lord Esher and is called the Margary quadrangle.

From its foundation in 1314 by Walter de Stapeldon, Bishop of Exeter, until the great benefaction of Sir William Petre (father of Dorothy Wadham) in 1566, the College existed on a narrow basis. It was for thirteen scholars nominated by the Dean and Chapter of Exeter and the income was provided by the tithes of the rectory of Gwinear in Cornwall to which the Bishop soon added those of Long Wittenham in Berkshire. Eight of the scholars were to be from Devon and four from Cornwall and one other was to be chaplain. They had to be of at least two years' standing

---

[1] See *V.C.H. Oxfordshire*, iii. 116.

and they elected their own successors. Only the chaplain was permanent, the others being unable to hold their Fellowship or scholarship for more than fourteen years. The Rectors were elected annually and there were ninety-seven between 1318 and 1556. The consequence was that the community was usually very young and discipline was not easy to maintain: the average age was perhaps twenty-five.[1] With commons at 10d. a week, the Rector and chaplain each got £3. 3s. 4d. a year and the Fellows £2. 13s. 4d. In 1408 commons was raised to 1s.

Sir William Petre, with the permission of Queen Elizabeth I and the Bishop of Exeter, Visitor of the College, effected a great change by founding in 1566 seven new Fellowships. Henceforward Rectors were to be elected for life and the Fellows similarly, except that they had to resign on marriage or when in receipt of an external income of more than ten marks a year. To the Rectorship was also attached the living of Kidlington. Commoners and battellars (paying members) were now admitted and the College increased its numbers from 91 in 1572 to 183 in 1612. It had a series of able Rectors, the greatest of whom was John Prideaux, 1612–42, and under him the College flourished as never before. It fell on bad days during and after the Civil War and the slump continued till the nineteenth century.

The west-country connexion is maintained by the fifteen or so Stapeldon Scholars who must have been born or educated there and, as at Pembroke and Jesus, a link with the Channel Islands is provided by the King Charles I scholarships for boys from there.

Famous men: Sir John Eliot; William Strode; Anthony Ashley Cooper, first Earl of Shaftesbury; Thomas Secker, Archbishop of Canterbury; Sir Edward Burne-Jones; William Morris; Sir Hubert Parry, Bt.; Sir Ray Lankester; Sir W. M. Ramsay; Don Salvador de Madariaga; Archbishop Lord Fisher of Lambeth; J. R. R. Tolkien.

Next to Exeter, beyond Brasenose Lane (the only street in Oxford that still preserves the medieval middle gutter or 'kennel') is

[1] *V.C.H. Oxfordshire*, iii. 108.

LINCOLN COLLEGE

Founded 1427. Present strength: The Rector; 22 Fellows; 5 Research Fellows; 17 lecturers; 42 scholars; 39 exhibitioners; 227 other members receiving tuition or supervision. *Buildings*: Front quadrangle, *c.* 1437–1479 (hall modernized 1791); kitchen, *c.* 1436–7; Chapel quadrangle, west range 1608–9; chapel and east range, 1629–31; Grove Building, 1880–2 (additions 1950); library, 1906–7; Rector's Lodging, 1929–30.

 'THE College of the Blessed Mary and All Saints, Lincoln, in the University of Oxford, commonly called Lincoln College' was founded in 1427 by Richard Fleming, Bishop of Lincoln, with the express purpose of training graduates in Theology to confute the Wyclifite heresies. Endowments were provided by the union of the three churches of All Saints', St. Michael's, and St. Mildred's, for which the Bishop got the King's permission. St. Mildred's was pulled down and the first part of the College was built on its site. It was the permanent duty of the College to provide chaplains for the other two churches and these livings are still in its gift.

There were to be a Rector and seven Fellows or scholars and the first buildings were where the front quadrangle still is. The site was gradually extended southwards and by 1772 it reached the churchyard of All Saints'.

The endowment can have amounted to little more than £15 a year after paying for the two chaplains and the maintenance charges on the two churches and was so far from sufficient that Thomas Rotheram (1423–1500), Bishop of Lincoln, reckoned as the second Founder, got Edward IV's permission to impropriate for the College the churches of Twyford in Buckinghamshire and Combe in Oxfordshire. He also gave the College a code of statutes which laid it down that all Fellows must come from one or other of the three dioceses of Lincoln, York, and Wells; that they must normally be of at least M.A. standing; that all must be priests or become such within a year and then read for the higher degrees of B.D. and D.D.

During the next century or so the College received numerous benefactions as a result of which it became the owner, among other properties, of Iffley mill (burnt down in 1908) and of the 'Mitre Hotel'. Its greatest benefactor was Nathaniel, Lord Crewe, later Bishop of Durham, who was first a Fellow and then Rector from 1668 till 1672. In 1717 he gave the College £474. 6s. 8d. a year to increase the incomes of all its members and to found twelve exhibitions of £20 apiece. Since the Royal commission of 1855 territorial qualifications for Fellowships have been abolished.

The buildings of Lincoln are modest but have all the charm of simplicity and the Turl Street front is most attractive. The construction of the gate-tower and the south part of the west range was possibly completed before Fleming's death, in January 1431. John Forest, Canon and Prebendary of Lincoln and Dean of Wells, continued the work and by 1437 most of the first quadrangle was completed. The chapel was on the first floor in the east part of the north range and was used until the present chapel was consecrated in 1631. In 1655 it became the library and in 1906 was divided into college rooms. Below it were two sets of rooms which became the Senior Common Room in 1662 and acquired its present panelling in 1684. The first library was at the west end of the north range, also on the first floor.

The hall has stood since 1437 and presents something like its original appearance. The fire-place dates from 1699 (restored 1891) but the octagonal louvre is still in position, the only one of the period surviving in Oxford. The panelling was the gift of Lord Crewe in 1701.

In 1470 the Rector left the gate-tower and lived in new Lodgings built at the south end of the hall with the bequest of Thomas Beckington, Bishop of Bath and Wells, and in 1479 Rotheram built the south side of the quadrangle.

In 1608 the west side of the second quadrangle was begun by Sir Thomas Rotheram, Founder's kin and Fellow, 1586–93. John Williams, Bishop of Lincoln, helped to finish the quadrangle and in particular, the chapel, which was consecrated in 1631. It is an excellent example of Jacobean Gothic, with fine seventeenth-century glass of Bernard van Linge, admirably carved stalls and screen, and a richly panelled ceiling which was repaired and recoloured in 1958.

In 1824 the Turl Street front was given battlements, which was a pity; they were also added to the quadrangles in 1852 but have now been removed.

Lincoln's most recent buildings have been those in the Grove, by Sir T. G. Jackson, 1880–2, to which a fourth floor was added in 1950: they are near the medieval kitchen; the new library, 1906–7, built in the garden, and the fine new house for the Rector (Herbert Read), 1930, facing the street. In 1939 the insatiable and regrettable craving of all colleges to grow bigger led Lincoln across the street where Sir Hubert Worthington and G. T. Gardner built sets of rooms over rent-producing shops.

At the Reformation Lincoln was, not surprisingly, firmly attached to the old religion and its Rectors were turned out in quick succession as well as most of the Fellows. The College did not recover till the days of Laud. Among the eight Fellows elected in 1606 was Robert Sanderson, of whom it is recorded: 'As a student he was remarkable, for he read regularly eleven hours a day; his compendium of logic was still studied in Oxford at the end of the eighteenth century; his character and piety fitted him for the part of mediator between the opposing parties in the church, though unfortunately his efforts were without success. He has left an enduring mark in the service of the Church of England in the stately eloquence of the Introduction to the Prayer Book ('It hath been the wisdom of the Church of England') which was written by him.'[1]

The golden age of Lincoln followed the reign of Crewe. Dr. John Radcliffe was a Fellow for a time (1669–77) and John Wesley became one in 1726. It was during his nine years at Lincoln that his ideas on religious discipline and devotion took shape. The college declined as the eighteenth century wore on, but revived under the stimulus of the morose and miserable, but powerful Mark Pattison, who, having been scholar and Fellow, became Rector (1861–84).

Famous men: Sir William Davenant; Robert Sanderson, Bishop of Lincoln; Nathaniel, third Lord Crewe, Bishop of Durham; John Wesley (Fellow); Mark Pattison; John, Viscount Morley.

[1] J. Wells, *Oxford and its Colleges* (3rd ed., 1899), p. 135.

At the corner of Turl Street and the High Street stands the Church of ALL SAINTS' destined (1971) to become the library of Lincoln College. It was designed by Henry Aldrich, Dean of Christ Church, and built in 1707–10 in succession to a medieval church. The spire was the work of Hawksmoor. When St. Martin's Church at Carfax was pulled down in 1892, the parish was amalgamated with All Saints', which thus became the City Church.

THE MITRE HOTEL dates mainly from the seventeenth century, about 1630, and has contemporary panelling and stairs. Part of the vaulted cellars is thirteenth-century. Having, however, no room for guests' motor cars, it had to close except for meals and since 1968 the upper floors accommodate Lincoln undergraduates.

If we turn back up Turl Street we shall find on our left, opposite Exeter College

JESUS COLLEGE

Founded 1571. *Present strength*: The Principal; 35 Fellows; 7 lecturers; 49 scholars; 65 exhibitioners; 272 B.A.s and commoners. *Buildings*: gatehouse, 1571 (altered); chapel, 1621; hall, 1617; library, 1679; first quadrangle, 1571–1621; second quadrangle, 1639–1713; Ship Street buildings, 1905; Old Members' Building, 1971. The east front on Turl Street was remodelled in 1756 and in 1865.

LETTERS patent for the foundation of a college for a Principal, eight Fellows, and eight scholars were issued in June 1571 by Queen Elizabeth I at the instance of Dr. Hugh Price. Price secured the site of White Hall, standing between Ship Street and Market Street, and he was able to build the south-east corner of the College before he died in 1574. Then difficulties arose because no statutes had been made and the endowment was inadequate. The College did not really thrive until after 1621, when Sir Eubule Thelwall became Principal. Statutes were approved in 1622 and sundry benefactions were received. Thelwall died in 1630 and was succeeded by Francis Mansell, 'perhaps the greatest of its Principals', under whom

29. Turl Street, with
Lincoln College and
All Saints' Church

30. Jesus College:
second quadrangle

31. Trinity College: South view of Chapel

many benefactions were received, particularly of lands in Wales. Charles I endowed a Channel Islands Fellowship. The loyalty of the College is adduced by the portraits of Charles I (studio of Van Dyck) and Charles II (attributed to Lely) in the hall.

In 1648 the Parliamentary Visitors ejected Mansell and almost all the 'foundation', but Mansell returned in 1652 and was reinstated as Principal in 1660, only to be succeeded in 1661 by Sir Leoline Jenkins. Jenkins resigned in 1673 and at his death left all his estates to the College, thus qualifying for the description of second Founder. They were worth about £700 a year and some of the property in London became immensely valuable later on. The Fellows and scholars continued to be drawn very largely from Wales and this tendency was further strengthened by the large Meyricke benefaction of 1713 for scholarships. Never numerous, the College sank to very low levels during the nineteenth century, but after the recommendations of the Second Royal Commission, 1882, when all Fellowships were thrown open, it made a spectacular revival in numbers and scholarship. Sir John Rhys, Principal 1895–1915, was a great scholar and under him the College took the initiative in the scientific field, opening its own chemistry laboratory under D. L. Chapman in 1908.

The College was about half Welsh in 1914 but now, though the Welsh connexion remains strong and highly valued, only about 15 to 20 per cent. of undergraduates come from Welsh schools.

Shortage of money meant that the building was piecemeal, yet it shows a surprising uniformity. We have seen that the first part was at the corner of Turl Street and Market Street. The hall followed in 1617 in good Jacobean Gothic, with a fine screen. Unfortunately the open hammer-beam roof was ceiled in in 1741, so that extra rooms might be made above. There are some good portraits. In 1621 the chapel was consecrated. The screen dates from 1693, but much of the interior was ruined by the Victorian Goths in 1864. The Principal's Lodgings, with a gloriously panelled drawing-room were built by Thelwall: the second quadrangle was built between 1639 and 1713 and the present library was opened in 1679, its fittings coming from its predecessor of the 1620's. It has a seventeenth-century gallery. The east front was remodelled in the Palladian style in 1756, but was regothicized and the tower built, by Buckler, in 1855.

The Ship Street range was built in 1906–8 including the laboratories which were closed in 1947, when the University had made other arrangements for teaching Chemistry, and turned into sets of rooms for undergraduates.

The latest building, opened by the Prince of Wales in June 1971, is brilliantly conceived and gives an air of spaciousness in a narrow place behind the second quadrangle. With a music room and seminar rooms, there are sets for twenty-four undergraduates.

Famous men: Lancelot Andrewes, Bishop of Winchester (from Cambridge); Henry Vaughan; Sir Leoline Jenkins; Sir Watkin Williams Wynn, 3rd Bt.; Thomas Charles, of Bala; William Lloyd, one of the Seven Bishops; Richard ('Beau') Nash; J. R. Green; T. E. Lawrence, 'of Arabia'; Viscount Sankey, Lord Chancellor; Harold Wilson, Prime Minister.

Across Broad Street and exactly opposite the end of Turl Street are the gates of

TRINITY COLLEGE

Founded 1555. *Present strength*: The President; 25 Fellows; 1 Visiting Fellow; 3 Junior Research Fellows; 12 lecturers; 32 scholars; 37 exhibitioners; 186 other members receiving tuition or supervision. *Buildings*: cottages, late seventeenth century, rebuilt; chapel, 1691–4; hall, 1618; library, 1417; Garden quadrangle, 1665–82; Kettell Hall, *c.* 1620; President's Lodging, 1885–7; New Buildings, 1883–5; New Library, 1925–8; Dolphin Gatehouse (facing St. Giles'), 1948; Cumberbatch quadrangle, 1968.

 THE core of Trinity is the site and buildings of the former Durham College, founded in 1286 by the Prior and Convent of Durham as a place where their monks could live while studying at Oxford. When the monasteries were suppressed by Henry VIII, the life went out of Durham College despite the efforts of the new Dean and Chapter of Durham to keep it going.

Then for a few years the buildings were maintained as a private hall, but in 1555 they were bought by Sir Thomas Pope, an eminently successful civil servant. He put them in order and in May 1556 installed the first President of Trinity with twelve Fellows and eight scholars, with letters patent granted by King Philip and Queen Mary. The greater part of the endowments were properties in Oxfordshire, including Wroxton Priory, and the rectory of Garsington was attached to the Presidency until 1871.

Commoners were admitted from the beginning and included an infusion of the landed gentry, for there has always been a tradition at Trinity in favour of 'good county families'. The College was fortunate in two early Presidents, Ralph Kettell, 1599–1643, and Ralph Bathurst, 1664–1704. Under them the College was popular and recruited young men who later achieved distinction either in Church or State. Pressure of numbers also caused gradual transmutation and expansion of the buildings.

Durham College, the original Trinity, lay well back from Broad Street and was approached by a narrow walled lane like that which still exists at Jesus College, Cambridge. It led straight through an arch at the west end of the chapel into the quadrangle. As we enter the quadrangle today we see, to our right, the east range, 1417–21, containing the old library on the first floor, with some old glass in the windows; the rest of the range was the President's Lodgings until the new house was built for him east of the chapel in 1885–7. The 'cock lofts' in the roof were inserted to accommodate commoners in 1602. Opposite to us is the recently refaced range which William Townsend rebuilt in 1728. It is singularly lacking in the grace of style usually characteristic of the period. On our left is the hall in Jacobean Gothic. It was built by Kettell in 1618 when its predecessor fell down: the interior was modernized in 1774 and its ceiling was tastefully restored in 1960. It contains portraits both interesting and good. Behind us, to our right, is the chapel. It was built by Bathurst in 1691—possibly to the designs of Dean Aldrich, with perhaps advice from Wren. Its predecessor, built in 1406, had become ruinous. The interior, with its magnificently carved reredos, stalls, and screen, is perfect and the hand of Grinling Gibbons has been seen in it. On the ceiling is a painting of the Ascension by Paul Berchet. In the corner north of the altar is the tomb, with effigies, of the Founder and his wife. The tower contains two rooms intended for the Dean and is crowned at the corners by statues representing Theology, Medicine, Geometry, and Astronomy.

The Garden quadrangle, which is open eastwards to the garden, is beyond Durham quadrangle. The north side (completed by 1668) was designed by Wren, when numbers were increasing under Bathurst. It was a delightful isolated block in the French Renaissance style and had two main stories with a pediment and a mansard roof with dormers. Its design was ruined by the addition of a full-scale third story in 1802. In 1682 the west side of the quadrangle was filled in, and here also the third story is modern.

We may enter the garden, which was completed in 1713 when the lime walk was planted, and, looking back, we see the charming irregularity of the roofs and chimneys of the surviving Durham buildings. Turning to the right we find ourselves in the front quadrangle with the President's house to our right and the New Buildings, both by Sir T. G. Jackson, R.A., to our left. Beyond the New Buildings is Kettell Hall, built by Kettell *c.* 1620 on Oriel property as an investment. Though it was used for commoners in the seventeenth century it was later let as a private house and not fully brought into the College until 1898. Behind the New Buildings are the War Memorial Library and the lively Cumberbatch quadrangle (architects: Robert Maguire and Keith Murray).

Surprisingly, Trinity has access, through the old 'Dolphin Inn' yard to St. Giles', and its Dolphin Gatehouse, by Sir Hubert Worthington, divides Balliol from St. John's.

Famous men: Henry Ireton; Edmund Ludlow; Gilbert Sheldon, Archbishop of Canterbury; John Aubrey; John, Lord Somers, Lord Chancellor; George Calvert, founder of Maryland; Thomas Warton; William Pitt, first Earl of Chatham; James, first Earl Stanhope; first Lord Baltimore; Frederick, Lord North, Prime Minister; W. S. Landor; J. H. Newman, Cardinal; William Stubbs, Bishop of Oxford; Sir Arthur Quiller-Couch; Randall Davidson, Archbishop of Canterbury; James, Viscount Bryce;

James Elroy Flecker; Charles Gore, Bishop, and R. A. Knox, Fellows; F. M. Earl Alexander of Tunis, K.G.; Rayner, first Lord Goddard, Lord Chief Justice; Kenneth, Lord Clark of Saltwood.

Returning to Broad Street we should note the handsome wrought-iron gate given by Lord Guilford in 1737 and the view of All Saints' Church down Turl Street.
Next door to Trinity is

BALLIOL COLLEGE

Founded c. 1263. Present strength: The Master; 56 Fellows; 13 lecturers; 70 scholars; 47 exhibitioners; 426 other members receiving tuition or supervision. *Buildings*: gatehouse, 1866; chapel, 1856; hall, 1877; Upper Library, 1431 and *c*. 1480; Lower Library, formerly hall, early-fifteenth-century; east and south ranges of front quadrangle, 1867–9; Garden quadrangle, 1714, 1769, 1827, 1853, 1877, 1905, 1913, 1965, 1968–9.

JOHN BALLIOL, whose name indicates French extraction (Bailleul), was a powerful baron, holding lands on both sides of the Scottish border. He married Dervorguilla, a descendant not only of the kings of Scotland and St. Margaret, but through her, of the Saxon house and Alfred the Great. Balliol became involved in a dispute with the Bishop of Durham in 1254 and the penance prescribed included the maintenance of sixteen poor scholars in the University of Oxford. They were to get 8*d*. a week commons and a tenement was found for them outside the city wall and ditch where the present Master's house stands. We do not know precisely when the College began, but it was probably between 1263 and 1268. It was, however, certainly the first to be a going concern, though its existence was tenuous and insecure for many years. Balliol died in 1269, but his widow continued the payments, and in 1282 she issued a charter which is still in the possession of the College. By this the scholars were to elect a Principal from among themselves but were to be subject to two external Masters, a Franciscan and a secular, who were to manage the property. The scholars were to be students in Arts.

99

One of the earliest endowments was the rectory of St. Lawrence Jewry, which the College held from 1294 until 1952. In 1304 it received Burnel's Inn, one of the private halls, standing west of where Peckwater quadrangle, Christ Church, is now. Sir Philip de Somervyle increased the endowment in 1340 and the great John Wyclif was Master perhaps from *c.* 1356 to 1361, but the College did not free itself from external control until 1507 when Richard Fox, Bishop of Winchester and Founder of Corpus, acting for the Pope, recast the statutes. The College was henceforth to be self-governing with a Master and ten Fellows and ten scholars who were not to be over eighteen on admission and each of whom was to be nominated by one of the Fellows, to whom he became servant. Furthermore, the College was given the unique privilege, which it still enjoys, of electing its own Visitor, who, incidentally, was to come to the College only once a year unless specially invited.

Meanwhile, in the middle of the fifteenth century, Balliol had been the resort of some distinguished leaders of the Renaissance, including George Neville, Archbishop of York and brother of Warwick 'the Kingmaker'; John Free, the first Englishman to become a professional humanist; and, above all, William Gray, Bishop of Ely, who died in 1478, and whose coat of arms can still be seen under the beautiful oriel window in the Master's Lodgings, south of the old hall (now the College library). One hundred and eighty-one of his original collection of 200 manuscript volumes still remain, and they comprise 'by far the finest, as well as the largest, private collection to survive in England from the Middle Ages'.[1]

Membership of the College was not much affected by the Reformation. We know that it was decreed in 1571 that commoners were to be assigned to tutors and required to do the same work as scholars. Fellow-commoners were admitted from 1610, which must have eased the financial position, and the number of undergraduates went up from about forty in 1580 to about seventy in 1641. Until 1601, except for two exhibitions for boys from the diocese of

[1] R. W. Hunt in *V.C.H. Oxfordshire*, iii. 82.

Worcester, Balliol scholarships had no local connexions, but in that year the College accepted the offer of Peter Blundell of Tiverton to found one scholarship and one Fellowship to be held only by boys from the school he set up there. The holder of the scholarship was to have the right to succeed to the Fellowship, which he might hold for ten years. In 1615 a potentially dangerous step was taken when it was laid down that if a Fellowship were not available when a Blundell scholar took his B.A., he should get the next vacancy on the old foundation.

The Civil War had as bad an effect upon Balliol as upon other colleges and after the Restoration the numbers continued low and debts grew. An appeal for help brought in some large subscriptions including one of £295 from Christ Church, but nearly £600 was still owing when, in 1674, the College accepted two Scottish exhibitions declined by Magdalen and in 1676, more dangerously, accepted £600 from the Blundell trustees on condition of maintaining another Blundell scholar and Fellow and suppressing one on the old foundation. The evil of this step was apparent in 1732 when out of fourteen Fellows, seven were from Blundell's school and 'the Visitor intimated, with some plainness of language, his conviction that they habitually voted for their compatriots without regard to the more important questions of good conduct and scholarship. Balliol [he said] was fast degenerating into a county college.'[1] Another local connexion, however, was to bring a succession of able men to the college. John Snell left money to provide two exhibitioners from the University of Glasgow and the first election was made in 1699.

Despite the receipt of numerous benefactions the eighteenth century was a depressing time for Balliol and its buildings fell into a bad state. Towards the end of the century, however, three non-Balliol men were elected into Fellowships, two from Brasenose, and one, John Parsons, 1785, from Wadham, who was destined to become Master in 1798 and to qualify for the description of 'the founder of modern Balliol'. With Eveleigh, Provost of Oriel, who also

[1] H. W. C. Davis, *Balliol College* (revised edition), 1963, p. 158.

came from Wadham, and Cyril Jackson, Dean of Christ Church, he was author of the new *University Statutes* (1800) which established the modern system of examinations for Honours degrees, and in 1808 the long tale of Balliol Firsts in the Schools began.

Parsons, who had become Dean of Bristol in 1810 and Bishop of Peterborough in 1813, continued as Master till his death in 1819. During his last twelve years nine out of fourteen Fellowship vacancies on the old foundation were filled by outsiders who had distinguished themselves in the Schools, but were not eligible for Fellowships in their own colleges.[1]

Another great Master, Richard Jenkyns, ruled Balliol from 1819 till 1854. Under him, in 1828, all the scholarships, except those on the Blundell and Snell foundations, were thrown open to competition and Jenkyns skilfully fostered good relations with the leading public schools. Dean Church said of him that he was 'an unfailing judge of a clever man, as a jockey might be of a horse'.[2] Fellows in his day were chosen 'with great discernment' and those elected in the thirties included A. C. Tait, W. G. Ward (from Lincoln), R. Scott (from Christ Church), W. C. Lake, and Benjamin Jowett. Tait is said to have been the first to break down the barrier between tutor and pupil and Jowett was a genius at eliciting and insisting upon hard work while preserving friendly relations. Jowett, at thirty-seven, was passed over for the Mastership in 1854 when Robert Scott was brought in from a country parsonage, but he became Regius Professor of Greek next year.

From 1856 all those admitted to Balliol were required to read for an Honours degree—no 'pass-men' were allowed, and in 1857, following the Royal Commission, the Blundell Fellowships were abolished and the Blundell scholarships increased to five. One of the last Blundell Fellows had been Frederick Temple, later Headmaster of Rugby, Archbishop of Canterbury, and father of another Balliol archbishop, William Temple. In 1867 the Brackenbury exhibitions were

[1] Hunt in *V.C.H. Oxfordshire*, iii. 85.
[2] Quoted by Hunt, ibid.

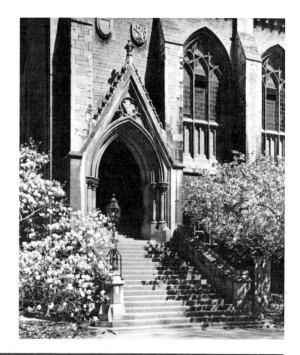

32. Balliol College:
entrance to hall

33. St. John's College:
Canterbury quadrangle

34. Ashmolean Museum and Taylorian Institution

founded and became a much-coveted award among the ablest boys from public and grammar schools.

When Jowett at length succeeded to the Mastership in 1870, he started weekly tutorial meetings to review the work of every undergraduate and in 1871 he set up an under-graduate library which was transferred to the old dining-hall when the new hall was opened in 1878. In his day the playing-field was acquired. In Holywell he built the first tutor's house, The King's Mound, and there several tutors' houses have since been erected. Finally Holywell Manor was bought and extended as an annexe in 1932. In all these respects Jowett's Balliol led the way and other colleges followed as they could, but even this was not all, for in 1879 the Balliol–Trinity laboratory was set up, and continued to do good work in Physical Chemistry until 1941 when the opening of the new University laboratory made the College effort superfluous. Since then a part of the laboratory has been adapted as a Balliol–Trinity science library.

Jenkyns, Jowett, and their successors brought a remark-able succession of young men from every sort of family and every sort of school, from the greatest to the humblest, to Balliol, and the Balliol influence in English public life since 1850 is incalculable. The number of Balliol men elected to Fellowships at other colleges must surely be far greater than any other college can show and certain it is that Balliol has a comfortable lead over all other colleges in the number of Firsts gained in the Final School Examinations since the Second World War.

Balliol's contribution to the architectural scene is less worthy. The only remains of the medieval College, apart from items in chapel and library, are the west range and half the north range of the front quadrangle. These include the old dining-hall, early-fifteenth-century, now the library, with part of the Master's house—note the oriel, which has been scrupulously restored—and the upper library, with rooms underneath, 1431 to c. 1480. Wyatt restored the inside of the library in 1792.

The Scottish-baronial façade, in the style of Balmoral, was built by Alfred Waterhouse in 1867–8 (the damage he did at Pembroke, Cambridge, was even worse, because what he destroyed there was more interesting and what he substituted is duller). The buildings he replaced here consisted of a fifteenth-century gate-tower, almost exactly like that at St. John's,[1] and a classical building to the east of it built early in the eighteenth century. They were undistinguished, perhaps, but not less charming than many Oxford fronts that we admire today and they were, at least, 'to scale'.

Facing us as we enter is the chapel, which is much better inside than the pink stripes of its exterior suggest. It is the work of Butterfield whose passion for patterns in walls had freer range at Keble. It was finished in 1857 and is the third chapel to stand on the site. The first was built c. 1309–28 and the second lasted from 1529 till 1856. Judging by the pictures it was a pleasant, Perpendicular edifice with large flat-arched windows and good seventeenth-century Renaissance reredos and stalls in oak. Much of its glass, including the east window, given by Lawrence Stubbs in 1529, two windows of Abraham van Linge 1637, and numerous older panels have survived to give pleasure in the present building, as have also the pulpit, c. 1630, and the lectern, c. 1635. The present stalls, original, plain, and good, date from 1937, when Butterfield's gothicisms were turned out. The altar frontal, part of the First World War Memorial, is silver-gilt repoussé work and striking in its richness.

A passage in the north-west corner of the quadrangle leads us between the door to the old hall and Salvin's tower, 1853, into the Garden quadrangle, which charms by its lawns, its trees, its irregular shape, and its extent. Immediately on our left are the Master's Lodgings (1867) and next door comes the Fisher Buildings (1769) and then, round the corner, a series of buildings along the street: Bristol, 1714; Basevi, 1826; Warren, including the Junior Common Room, 1913; Salvin, including the St. Giles' gate-tower, 1852. The modern buildings in the north-west corner (1968) are by G. J. Beard, as is the addition to the Senior Common Room at the far end of the hall (1965). The hall itself, and the part of the S.C.R. below it, were built by Waterhouse in

[1] Cf. the Loggan prints, 1675.

1877. The hall is good and contains a fine organ given by Jowett, in whose day the famous fortnightly Balliol concerts began.

Famous men: Richard Fitz Ralph, Archbishop of Armagh; William Gray, Bishop of Ely; George Neville, Archbishop of York; Cuthbert Tunstall, Bishop of Durham; John Morton, Archbishop of Canterbury; John Evelyn; Adam Smith; Robert Southey; J. G. Lockhart; Matthew Arnold; A. H. Clough; A. C. Swinburne; T. H. Green; Andrew Lang; A. P. Stanley, Dean of Westminster; B. Jowett; A. C. Tait, Archbishop of Canterbury; Cardinal Manning; Frederick Temple, Archbishop of Canterbury; Henry Herbert Asquith, first Earl of Oxford and Asquith; Edward, Viscount Grey of Fallodon; Earl Loreburn, Lord Chancellor; Charles Gore, Bishop of Oxford; C. G. Lang, Archbishop of Canterbury; Arnold Toynbee; A. C. Bradley; George Nathaniel, Marquess Curzon of Kedleston; H. Belloc; R. A. Knox; Herbert, first Viscount Samuel; Sir Ernest Barker; R. H. Tawney; Lord Beveridge; H.M. the King of Norway; Harold Macmillan, Prime Minister; David, first Viscount Kilmuir, Lord Chancellor; Vincent Massey, Governor-General of Canada; Graham Greene; Edward Heath, Prime Minister; Sir Seretse Khama.

If we turn right on leaving Balliol and immediately right again we pass on our left St. Mary Magdalene's Church with a squat sixteenth-century tower. Although there is a quantity of medieval work surviving, the structure was heavily restored in the 1840's, when the north aisle was entirely rebuilt. Also on the left and north of the church stands the MARTYRS' MEMORIAL designed by Sir Gilbert Scott and erected in 1841 to commemorate Latimer, Ridley, and Cranmer, who were burned at the stake in Broad Street in 1555–6 for their adherence to the reformed Church of England in the reign of Mary Tudor. Continuing northwards, we come to

ST. JOHN'S COLLEGE

Founded 1555. *Present strength*: The President; 43 Fellows; 2 Fereday Fellows; 1 Woodhouse Fellow; 8 lecturers; 11 senior scholars; 57 scholars; 37 exhibitioners; 262 B.A.s and commoners. *Buildings*: first quadrangle begun 1437; chapel, 1530; old library, 1596; Laud's library, 1631-6; Canterbury quadrangle, 1631-6; north quadrangle, 1880, 1900, 1906, 1909, 1933, 1959; Dolphin quadrangle, 1948.

 T HE College of St. John Baptist was founded in the same year as Trinity, also in the surviving buildings of a monastic college and also by a prosperous Londoner. Sir Thomas White was a wealthy Merchant Taylor, a former Lord Mayor of London, and a devoted Roman Catholic, keen to do his best 'to strengthen the orthodox faith, in so far as it is weakened by the damage of time and the malice of men'.[1] Like Fleming, the Founder of Lincoln, his object was to secure a supply of clergy to rebut current heresies.

The site and buildings were those of St. Bernard's College, a Cistercian house begun by Archbishop Chichele in 1437 shortly before he went on to found All Souls. White bought them for a nominal sum from Christ Church, to which the Crown had assigned them at the Dissolution. The west front of the College was more or less as it is now, also the north and south sides of the quadrangle, but the east side where a library was building was still unroofed.

The dedication of the College was changed to 'St. John Baptist, the patron saint of tailors'. There were to be a President and fifty Fellows. The Fellows were to be on probation for two years—extended to three in 1566—after which they could remain Fellows for life, subject to their remaining bachelors, taking priests' orders, and not inheriting property worth more than £10 a year. Strict but self-defeating rules were made about compulsory residence. No one was to be away for more than sixty days in the year, except for urgent reasons, but, to deliver an important sermon a Fellow might have ten days' leave; for ordinary sermons, eight. As he could also claim another sixty days

[1] From the College statutes, quoted in *V.C.H. Oxfordshire*, iii. 251.

ex causis promotionis, a beneficed Fellow might well arrange to be away for a great part of the year and enjoy a fat living as well as his College stipend. Leave to travel abroad was also given.

White reserved a proportion of the fellowships for certain schools, notably Merchant Taylors' School (founded 1561), Christ's Hospital, and the schools at Tonbridge, Bristol, Reading, and Coventry. To this day, of the forty-six entrance scholarships, fifteen are appropriated to Merchant Taylors', almost as many as New College allots to Winchester, and more than Christ Church gives to Westminster. But it is a great thing for a school to have an assured way into the University for its abler boys.

Though the College in time became rich, it had financial difficulties at first, particularly between the Founder's death in 1567 and his widow's in 1572. Then her life interests fell in and the College bought the Manor of Walton, comprising a great part of what is now north Oxford, as well as the advowson of St. Giles' Church and much neighbouring property. These were destined to become a gold mine in the nineteenth century. The College also acquired Bagley Wood. It was not at full strength till 1583, but already it was over-full with commoners, paying their own way—indeed it was two to a bed for all under sixteen, even though attics were built over the south and west sides of the quadrangle.

In its early days the College was not happy in religion and there were numerous defections to Roman Catholicism, notably by the brilliant young Edmund Campion, who had spoken the Founder's funeral oration and received Queen Elizabeth I with a Latin speech. He was martyred at Tyburn in 1581.

The greatest days of the College came in the first half of the seventeenth century under the Presidencies of William Laud 1611–21, William Juxon 1621–33, and Richard Baylie 1633–48 and 1660–7. All were devoted to their *alma mater*. Laud, destined to be Charles I's Archbishop of Canterbury, came up at sixteen as a commoner but within a month was nominated to the Reading close scholarship on its falling vacant. His great work for the College was done while he was Archbishop and Chancellor of the University. He built the east and north sides of Canterbury quadrangle in 1631–6 and thus gave the College a great extension to its library, an exquisite garden front, and two lovely Renaissance colonnades—for £5,500. The statues of Charles I and Henrietta Maria by le Sueur cost him £400. When it was all finished he gave the King a great banquet in the library and a play was performed in the hall. As is well known, Laud's attempts to enforce the strict observance of the Prayer Book and his consequent struggle with the Puritans eventually brought about his impeachment for high treason, and he was beheaded in 1645. In 1663 his body was brought from All Hallows-by-the-Tower and buried in St. John's chapel between those of Juxon and the Founder. Laud gave the College many advowsons and his gifts were handsomely supplemented by Sir William Paddy, who left the College £3,200 in 1635. During the Commonwealth and throughout the eighteenth century the College led an undistinguished existence, but contributed a fair share of eminent men to the national history.

A little has already been said of the buildings. The front is fifteenth-century and the figures over the gate are of St. Bernard, Archbishop Chichele, and the Founder. On the interior side of the gate the figure is of St. John Baptist, by Eric Gill, 1936.

The chapel was consecrated in 1530, but has been repeatedly altered, by the Founder, by Laud, at the Restoration, and, finally, by Blore in 1843. Fortunately the Baylie Chapel, 1662, was suffered to remain, with its fan-vault of plaster and its interesting tombs. The stone reredos and the east window are the work of C. E. Kempe, 1892.

The hall has also suffered many changes. Its ceiling dates from 1730; the marble chimney-piece from 1731, and the stone screen, by James Gibbs, replaced a wooden one in 1742. The panelling was done in 1744.

The south side of the Canterbury quadrangle was built as a library in 1596–8 and it is interesting that 1,000 loads of stone and timber used in its construction came from 'the great house' of the White Friars near Gloucester Hall at the west end of Beaumont St., which the College bought in 1595 for that very purpose. White Friars was the former Beaumont Palace of Kings Henry I and II. Incidentally, St. John's owned Gloucester Hall until it was acquired for Worcester College in 1713.

One of the greater glories of St. John's has always been its garden. The lawn is superb and both experts and amateurs will like to see Bidder's rock garden in the north-west corner.

The North quadrangle has been built in stages, 1880, 1900, 1909, 1933. In 1958 a new and original honeycomb design was adopted for extensions on the east side. These are in Portland stone, which is unusual in Oxford.

The Dolphin Building, by Sir Edward Maufe, R.A., to the south of the College was built in 1948.

Famous men: Edmund Campion; William Laud and William Juxon, Archbishops of Canterbury; R. Henley, first Earl of Northington, Lord Chancellor; James Shirley; A. E. Housman; George, Viscount Cave, Lord Chancellor; Gilbert Murray, O.M.; L. B. Pearson, Canadian Prime Minister; Dean Rusk, U.S. Secretary of State; Sir Tyrone Guthrie.

If we cross the road from St. John's and bear to the left we shall come to the TAYLOR INSTITUTION, often called the TAYLORIAN, after Sir Robert Taylor, an architect who died in 1788 and left his residuary estate of £65,000 for the teaching of modern languages at Oxford. The University got the money in 1835 and decided to combine in one building both this institute and a new gallery to house the overcrowded collections of the Old Ashmolean which had already overflowed into the Clarendon Building and the Bodleian Library. The result was the building which stands at the corner of Beaumont Street, opposite the Randolph Hotel. It was built in 1841–5 by C. R. Cockerell, R.A., in a mixture of Portland stone for the columns, pilasters, and entablatures and Box Ground (or Bath) stone for the rest, except the plinth, which is of Whitby stone and had weathered so badly that it had to be replaced in 1960–1. The east wing along St. Giles' is the Taylorian and contains a fine modern-language library and teaching rooms. Extensions northwards in 1932–8 include a fine lecture-room cum small theatre. The central range and the west wing, with extensions along Beaumont Street and behind are the ASH-MOLEAN MUSEUM in which is also accommodated the Ruskin School of Drawing.

This is not the place to catalogue the contents or to list the munificent benefactors, but the visitor will here find as representative a collection of the great masters of all periods of European painting as he will anywhere else in England outside London. There are not only some fine individual pictures such as Paolo Uccello's *A Hunt in a Forest* and Piero di Cosimo's *A Forest Fire*, but there are also one of the finest collections of Michelangelo and Raphael drawings in existence and an important collection of Dutch still-life paintings. Other notable groups are those of modern French paintings, including a room devoted to paintings by members of the Pisarro family, and another to the Pre-Raphaelites. There is also the unique Hope collection of engraved portraits, English and European. There is a great collection of silver of the seventeenth and eighteenth centuries, including especially work by Paul Lamerie and other Huguenots; communion plate from St. Mary the Virgin; and sixteenth-century German gold and silver plate. There are remarkable bronzes, ivories, sculptures, tapestries; seventeenth- and eighteenth-century miniatures, snuff boxes, and watches. There is the famous Hill collection of musical instruments and a collection of coins second only to that in the British Museum. There are the Pomfret and Arundel marbles and a great collection of antiquities from every age and all parts of Europe, including Crete, the Ægean, and Egypt. Among British antiquities the greatest treasure is, perhaps, the Alfred Jewel. The Department of Eastern Art is a colourful section of the Museum, in which the collection of Chinese ceramics is especially noteworthy.

On the south side of Beaumont Street, which was built in Bath stone *c*. 1820, is the PLAYHOUSE which, originating in the enthusiasm and hard work of numerous old members of O.U.D.S. in the 1920's, was built and largely financed by Eric Dance in 1936. In 1961 the lease was taken over by the University, which is now responsible for the theatre.

South side of quadrangle, the fifteenth-century *Mansions*

North side of quadrangle

35. Worcester College

36. Nuffield College

37. Somerville College:
front quadrangle

WORCESTER COLLEGE

Founded 1714. *Present strength*: The Provost; 34 Fellows; 10 lecturers; 1 Laycock Student of Egyptology; 3 senior scholars; 46 scholars; 53 exhibitioners; 257 other members receiving tuition or supervision. *Buildings*: chapel, *c.* 1720-91; hall, *c.* 1720-84; library, *c.* 1730; south range of cottages and Pump Quad and Senior Common Room range, north of Chapel, fifteenth-century; north range and Provost's Lodging, 1753-76; Nuffield block, 1938; Besse Building, 1954; New Building, 1961; Wolfson Building, 1971.

 SIR LAWRENCE JONES in his book *An Edwardian Youth*[1] says Worcester is a surprising college: 'I call it surprising because Worcester has a stern and haughty exterior that might have been painted by James Pryde, turning, despite the perfection of its proportions, a blank and discouraging stare upon the approaching visitor. But once inside the gate and under the heavy arcade, you get the most delectable of welcomes. A gracious, high-bred façade on your right looks down, indulgently, at a row of irregular and diminishing little houses on your left, with a lawn between; all is grace and intimacy; there is neither condescension on the right nor too much humility on the left. A narrow passage at the end of the little houses leads to wide lawns and great trees and a swan lake and I have known people who pretended to visit Worcester for the sake of these gardens. But lawns and trees and lakes are common enough; it is the three-sided quadrangle, and the sudden pleasure of the transition from heavy, almost sullen blankness to smiling graciousness that gives to Worcester her incomparable charm. She lies remote from the rest, but has grandeur and elegance enough to make her self-sufficient. It is deplorable to think that we called her "Wuggins".'

Worcester is the third of the existing colleges whose roots go back to a monastic foundation. In 1283 Sir John Giffard, by way of penance, gave his property in Oxford to Gloucester Abbey, but in 1298 the same property seems to have been regranted to the Benedictines of the Southern Province with the result that many abbeys besides Gloucester built their

[1] Pp. 94–95.

own quarters in Gloucester College and subscribed to the erection of a common hall, chapel, and library. With the Dissolution the College ended. It fell into various hands and narrowly missed being the palace of the new Bishop of Oxford. Much had been destroyed, however, including chapel and library, before it was bought by Sir Thomas White as a part of the endowment of St. John's. He repaired it as far as he could and set it up as a dependent hall, whose Principal should normally be a Fellow of St. John's paying rent to the parent college.[1] It saw good days and bad, but never really recovered after the Civil War, and in the Principalship of Dr. Byrom Eaton, 1662–92, membership seems to have dwindled almost to nothing. Luckily for him Eaton held numerous ecclesiastical preferments. His successor, Dr. Benjamin Woodroffe, a Canon of Christ Church, was an odd man who spent much money on the place, but it never really prospered and his project of turning it into a college for students of the Greek Church failed.

Meanwhile Sir Thomas Cookes, a Worcestershire baronet, had declared his intention of giving £10,000 for an Oxford college, to be connected with Bromsgrove School, which he had recently rehabilitated. There was considerable competition for the money. Cookes died in 1701 and Woodroffe —after a spell of imprisonment for debt in the Fleet—in 1711. In 1712 Richard Blechynden, D.C.L., a Canon of Gloucester, became Principal and Cookes's trustees decided to buy the Hall from St. John's and turn it into a college under the name of Worcester, for a Provost, six Fellows, and eight scholars. Blechynden continued as first Provost and reigned till 1736.

The buildings were in a deplorable state and the College was poor, but it had some good friends. In 1717 a Mrs. Alcorne bequeathed £800 and the front, as we know it, was begun. Hawksmoor was the architect and Dr. George Clarke of All Souls was a sort of godfather. He gave money and advice, founded more Fellowships and scholarships, and, on his death in 1736, bequeathed to the College all his books and manu-

[1] Cf. the relationship of Oriel and St. Mary Hall; Magdalen and Magdalen Hall, &c.

scripts, including a priceless collection of architectural drawings and some early plays. It was due to him that the great
classical north range (architects, Clarke and Henry Keene)
was begun. It was to have been extended to the street and been
paralleled on the south side, but it is just as well that this
proved financially impossible. As it was, building was slow.
The hall was not finished till 1784 or the chapel till 1791.

The library, over the cloister, is a fine long room, with
shelves and gallery on three sides and nine great windows
looking west. The hall, by James Wyatt, is unique in Oxford
in having a Corinthian colonnade at the west end. The
chapel, redecorated in 1863–4, is likewise remarkable, being
at once bright in colour but dimly lit: well worth seeing.

Most of the rest of the College survives from the fifteenth
century and though subjected to much tampering and
alteration it has kept its beauty. Of the row of cottages or
camerae on the south side, we know from the coat of arms
over the door that Malmesbury Abbey had the first: the
hall was here from 1720 till 1784. The next little house probably belonged to St. Augustine's, Canterbury, and the last
to Pershore Abbey. There used to be a similar range all
along the north side, but now only the east end of this
survives, hidden away behind the chapel. It contains the
Senior Common Room and may be seen from the Fellows'
garden. Incidentally the shields over the street door just to
the north of this range are those of Ramsey, St. Albans,
and Winchcombe Abbeys.

At the west end of the north range the monks of St.
Albans had their quarters, being next beyond Norwich;
it was here that the Principals lived after the Dissolution,
and here that the present palatial Lodgings of the Provosts
was built in the splendid and spacious style which is the
mark of the eighteenth century.

Tucked away to the south of the hall is Pump Quad. Most
of it belonged to Glastonbury, but the bit in the north-east
corner was part of Bury St. Edmunds. Its appearance was
spoiled in 1824 by the addition of the top story: and the
same may be said of the great north terrace building where
attics do violence to Keene's design.

If we go into the garden we get a picturesque view of the south side of the cottages and can pick out the old kitchen by its great chimney-stack. A new building (architect, W. G. Newton) to the east of the garden was erected in 1938 as a result of a gift of £50,000 from Lord Nuffield, who also founded medical scholarships, and a further new building, in brown brick (architect, Sir Hugh Casson) was completed in 1961, also at the east end of the garden. Between these is a third block opened in 1971 and designed by Peter Bosanquet. Another new block, the Besse Building (p. 129), was built in 1954 to the north of the Provost's stables and his old kitchens were turned into a War Memorial Hall in 1949. Worcester is the only Oxford college to have a lake and playing-fields in its immediate grounds.

Famous men: *Gloucester Hall*: Richard Lovelace; Sir Kenelm Digby; *Worcester College*: Thomas De Quincey; Sir W. H. Hadow.

From Worcester College, northwards, Walton Street will take us to RUSKIN COLLEGE, founded in 1899 as a place to which working men could come up to study for a year in what was then the scholarly quietude of Oxford. Its members usually read for the University Diploma in Economics and Political Science, and many of the abler ones have gone on to join a college and read for a degree.

A little farther on is the UNIVERSITY PRESS. The dignified, if austere, classical façade has a gateway in the middle leading to a pleasant, grassed quadrangle, with the printing works on three sides. On the fourth side, and separating the works from the street, are administrative and publishing offices.

This is the third home (cf. pp. 82, 86) of the 'public academic printing-office' which the University, spurred on by Archbishop Laud, bound itself by the Statute of 1634 to establish and maintain. It was built in 1826–32 in a district, then of orchards and small-holdings, known as 'Jericho', and led to further industrial development of the area. The designs for it were made by Daniel Robertson, and they had been so far carried out by the time of his death that Edward Blore, succeeding him as architect, was unable to convert them to Gothic. Printing in the new building began in 1829.

The early history of the Press was episodic. The first book published with the licence of the University, a commentary on the Apostles' Creed attributed to St. Jerome, is dated 1468; but this must be a slip for 1478, for it was not till 1477 that Caxton printed his first book at Westminster. The first Oxford Printer was one Theodoric Rood, of Cologne; but he, like his successors for more than 150 years, furnished his own capital and premises and used the University imprint much as a modern tradesman may use the royal warrant of appointment. The history of the Press as a continuous institution dates from the seventeenth century. Thanks to the intercession of Laud, the Royal Charters of 1632–6 gave the University the right to print and sell 'all manner of books' (including Bibles and Prayer Books), and in 1633 the Proctors first appointed 'Delegates for printing', of whom there has since been an almost uninterrupted succession sitting under the Chairmanship of the Vice-Chancellor. Laud's plans first bore fruit in 1668, when the Sheldonian Theatre was so far built that printing presses could be installed in it. The Delegates, however, did not find the management of the business easy, and in 1672 they were relieved of it by the famous Dr. Fell, Dean of Christ Church and subsequently Bishop of Oxford, who in that year began to print on their behalf in the Theatre. Fell made the reputation of Oxford printing, and the Press still holds the type which he collected and which still bears his name. Fell's executors surrendered his rights and equipment to the Delegates in 1690, and since then they have carried on printing and publishing in the name of the University.

The 'O.U.P.' is today one of the largest publishing houses in the world. It has, besides its principal establishments in Oxford, London, and New York, branches throughout the world. It remains a department of the University, if in some ways anomalous, and its policy is controlled in all its activities by the Delegates of the Press, a committee of nineteen dons including the Vice-Chancellor, Proctors, and Assessor *ex officio*. Their senior executive officer is the Secretary.

Other principal officers are the Deputy Secretary, who presides over the Clarendon Press Publishing Department at Oxford; the Printer to the University; the London Publisher and Manager, who is responsible for Bible publishing and other publishing departments in London as well as for all overseas offices with the exception of New York; and the Controller of the Wolvercote Paper Mill, which was acquired by the Delegates in 1872 and has been much extended since 1950. The Press has a long tradition of publishing learned books, and by its more profitable activities in other fields is enabled to publish many which cannot hope to pay their own way. It is perhaps particularly known for its Bibles, of which it prints more than 3 million every year, and for its dictionaries and other works of reference. Learned books printed at Oxford in the Delegates' own works and under the direct supervision of their officers are published under the imprint 'Oxford: at the Clarendon Press'; other books, whether published in Oxford, London, or elsewhere, bear the imprint 'Oxford University Press'. The name 'Clarendon Press', which is sometimes used to denote the printing works as well as the publishing department, derives from the Clarendon Building in Broad Street, which was the home of the Press between 1713 and 1829 and was itself named after the Earl of Clarendon, author of the Oxford best seller, *History of the Great Rebellion*.

ST. PAUL'S CHURCH, built in the classical Ionic style in 1836 by subscription on land given by the Press, is opposite. It has fallen into disuse and its future is uncertain.

ST. BARNABAS' CHURCH is at the bottom of Cardigan Street, by the canal wharf. It was built in the Byzantine style by Sir R. Blomfield in 1869 and holds a special place in the affections of those devoted to the High Church party. There are ten tubular bells.

If we return down Walton Street, leaving Worcester College on our right, there comes at once into view the new spire of

NUFFIELD COLLEGE

Founded 1937. *Present strength*: The Warden; 26 Fellows; 11 Visiting
Fellows; 14 Research Fellows; 53 students; 49 other members receiving
tuition or supervision. There are no undergraduates.

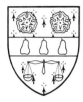 SIR WILLIAM RICHARD MORRIS, first
Viscount Nuffield, began life in humble cir-
cumstances and beginning with a small bicycle
shop developed a great motor manufacturing
business, the centre of which is at Cowley in
East Oxford. As an industrialist in Oxford he
was so impressed by the need of greater mutual
understanding between the academic and industrial and
commercial elements in modern society that he wrote to the
University in October 1937 offering to found a college 'to
encourage research especially but not exclusively in the field
of social studies, and especially by making easier the co-
operation of academic and non-academic persons'. Thus it is
that there are among the Fellows 'not more than twenty . . .
who shall be persons competent to assist those engaged in
the University in research by giving them the fruits of
their experience in practical affairs'. This group has so far
included chairmen of great industrial concerns, former
members of the Cabinet and Civil Service, Trade Union
leaders, a speaker of the House of Commons, an Adviser to
the Bank of England, and the Chairman of the Atomic
Energy Authority. The College has already been responsible for a great deal of research, the results of which have
been published in its name.

It was the first college in the University to which both
men and women were admitted, but its example has since
been followed by Linacre, St. Cross, and Wolfson.

The buildings, designed by Messrs. Harrison, Barnes,
& Hubbard, make a picturesque group of gabled Cotswold roofs, with St. Peter's College in its Neo-Georgian
red-brick with stone facings and classical balustrading on
the bluff behind and the Castle mound raising its steep green
slope to the south. They stand on low-lying ground, the site
of the old canal wharf and former Castle mill. Their design

117

is simple and depends for its effect upon its just proportions. It is at once traditional and original. In one respect only is there an exciting breakaway from the conventional. The great tower holds books, not bells, and the copper-clad spire, rising to 141½ ft., is a secular contribution to the sky-line. The room at present used as a Chapel is at the top of a staircase in the lower quadrangle. It was designed by John Piper and has accommodation for forty people. The floor, the stalls, the altar are in black and white. The glass in the north window was made by Patrick Reyntiens to a design of John Piper and shows the Five Wounds of Christ. The library is embellished with paintings of *The Four Seasons*, Spring and Winter by Derrick Greaves and Summer and Autumn by Edward Middleditch.

The main part of the buildings, including hall and spire, were finished in 1958, the foundation stone having been laid by the then Chancellor of the University, the late Earl of Halifax, K.G., in the presence of the Founder, on 21 April 1949.

During the period before the completion of the buildings the College occupied various houses in north Oxford.

To the south of Nuffield College is a group of county buildings, including the Castle, the jail, the County Hall, the Assize Court, and the Education Offices.

THE CASTLE was built by Robert d'Oilly, one of the Conqueror's men, in 1071, and the chapel of St. George whose tower and crypt are all that remain, apart from the mound, dates from 1074. The Castle area was extensive and its situation strong. Old plans show six towers round the peri-meter and a ten-sided keep on the top of the mound, with a well. The only time when it played any part in national history was when King Stephen besieged his rival, Matilda, in it for three months in 1142. She was at last forced to escape, clad in white, so it is said, over the ice and snow to Wallingford and the Castle surrendered at once. Of its subsequent history little is known, but it appears to have been in a ruinous state in 1331.

The church of ST. THOMAS THE MARTYR is near the station.

3. St. Anne's Hall:
dining-hall

4. Lady Margaret Hall:
the new library
on the right

40. Keble College: chapel

Its chancel is twelfth-century, but the nave was rebuilt in 1500 when the tower was added. It has six bells. There is a fine brass candelabrum dated 1705.

HYTHE BRIDGE takes its name from the hythes or quays which used to line the river here and where, among other things, Cotswold stone and timber for college building was unloaded, having come down from Radcot Bridge or Eynsham.

Standing above Nuffield College and between Bulwarks Lane and New Inn Hall Street (once called the Street of the Seven Deadly Sins) is

ST. PETER'S COLLEGE

Founded 1928. *Present strength*: The Master; 28 Fellows; 3 lecturers; 41 scholars; 28 exhibitioners; 242 other members receiving tuition or supervision.

THE College of St. Peter-le-Bailey stands on the site of one of the most ancient medieval halls, Trilleck's Inn, which became New Inn Hall on being rebuilt *c.* 1476. This Hall became a resort of lawyers and had a succession of distinguished Principals, including two Regius Professors of Civil Law and the University's first M.P. It was markedly Puritan before the Civil War and during the war Charles I set up his mint there for turning college plate into money. After the Restoration it again had a number of distinguished Principals, including Sir William Blackstone and Sir Robert Chambers, but its membership was never large. Its best period in the nineteenth century was under J. A. Cramer, 1831–47, who was Regius Professor of History and Public Orator, and who built what later became Hannington Hall and is now the dining-hall.

In 1887 New Inn Hall was absorbed in Balliol in accordance with the prescription of the Commissioners of 1881.

The nucleus of St. Peter's was the Church of St. Peter-le-Bailey and the rectory house, to which was added Cramer's block.

The church was moved to its present site only in 1874. Until then it stood where the public garden now is at the south corner of the street. Much of the old building was incorporated in the new, including many memorials and even some twelfth-century corbels which may be seen in the tower porch. Basil Champneys was the architect.

The rectory was built by the Canal Company in 1797 and was bought for the church in 1878 by Canon Henry Linton, rector. From 1879 to 1899 Dr. F. J. Chavasse, later Bishop of Liverpool, was rector and when he retired in 1923 he found the old house vacant, for the living was then being held in plurality with St. Ebbe's. He came to live there and conceived the idea of a new college which was specially to cater for poorer men and for those who might seek orders in the Church of England. He died in 1928 before his idea could be realized, but others took it up, notably his own surviving son, who became the first Master,[1] and Lord Nuffield, who gave £50,000.

The parish church became the College chapel (as St. John's Church had become Merton Chapel); the former rectory, now called Linton House, provided room for the library on the first floor; and Hannington Hall, named after the first bishop of Eastern Equatorial Africa, a D.D. and member of St. Mary Hall (see p. 29) who was murdered by natives of Uganda in 1885.

The first of the new buildings, designed by R. Fielding-Dodd, were the Emily Morris and Besse blocks. A further new building was opened in 1971 by Edward Akufo-Addo, President of Ghana, an old member of the College, and an east wing is now (1971) under construction.

On the other side of Bulwarks Lane, close to Nuffield, is the former 'Canal House', stone-built, Georgian, erected in 1828, which became the Master's Lodging in 1959.

Plans have been drawn up by the distinguished American architect, Professor R. Buckminster Fuller, for an underground theatre to seat 200 and to be named after Samuel Beckett. To this end Mr. S. J. Zacks of Toronto gave $175,000.

[1] C. M. Chavasse, Bishop of Rochester, 1940-60.

Turning left from St. Peter's College, we may go along New Inn Hall Street, and on our right into St. Michael's Street, in which stands the main entrance to

THE OXFORD UNION SOCIETY, the largest and the oldest undergraduate club, which may also be reached through Frewin Court, by Woolworth's. It consists of a comfortable series of club rooms including a dining-room and bar, a billiard room, and rooms for receptions and dances in the basement. But the principal features are the debating-hall and the library of over 50,000 books.

Clubs of all kinds are characteristic of undergraduate life in Oxford. There are social clubs such as 'Vincent's' (for Blues and others who have distinguished themselves at games) and the Gridiron; the Oxford University Dramatic Society and the Experimental Theatre Club for those keen on acting, and a host of religious, philosophical, political, historical, artistic, musical, and literary clubs. But the largest, most comprehensive, and oldest is the Union Society.

It arose out of that stirring of political thought which began in the eighteenth century and, continuing through the French Revolution, produced the modern democratic era. Oxford has always produced politicians, but never so many as it has done since the Union began in 1823. At first it was frowned upon as likely to be subversive and dangerous, but the authorities had no cause to fear, for though it stood for the free discussion of every sort of idea except theological, it was essentially aristocratic.

To begin with, it met in rooms in Christ Church. Its first President, D. Maclean of Balliol, became M.P. for Oxford, and of its earliest leaders nine were sons of peers and almost all achieved some eminence in Parliament, in the Church, the Foreign Service, or the Law. As it began, so it went on. From 1829 till 1854 it met in Wyatt's rooms in High Street, but in 1852 it acquired its present site. The first debating-hall, now the library, was built by Benjamin Woodward in 1854. Its upper walls and ceiling were covered with frescoes by D. G. Rossetti, with the help of Burne-Jones and others, depicting scenes from the *Morte d'Arthur*, but as the plaster was not properly prepared they have not lasted well. In

1878 a new and larger debating-hall was built by Alfred Waterhouse and its predecessor became the main library. The latest building (1910), by Mills & Thorpe, contains the new library below and dining and club rooms above, together with a house for the Steward.

In the debating-hall are busts of W. E. Gladstone, Lord Salisbury, Lord Oxford and Asquith, Lord Curzon, Lord Birkenhead, Lord Simon, and Mr. Macmillan, all of them, except the last, Presidents of the Society in their undergraduate days: Mr. Macmillan held all the other offices in turn until Christmas 1914 after which the Union's normal activities were suspended until 1919.

Continuing along St. Michael's Street we come into Cornmarket Street almost immediately opposite the tower of ST. MICHAEL-AT-THE-NORTH-GATE. It was a part of the city-wall defences and adjoined the gate over which was *Bocardo*, the prison. It was here that the bishops, Latimer, Ridley, and later Cranmer, were held before their burning at the stake in Broad Street: a cross in the road marks the spot.

The tower, like the city wall, is built of 'random rubble', and dates from early in the eleventh century and is the oldest building in the city. The small round-headed windows with the single baluster and some characteristic 'long and short' work show it to be Saxon. The chancel dates from the thirteenth century and most periods of architecture are represented. Most notable are panels of thirteenth-century glass in the east window. The pulpit is fifteenth-century. There is some fine plate, including a cup of 1562 and a seventeenth-century chest. The six bells are seventeenth- and eighteenth-century.

On the corners opposite St. Michael's Church there are two pleasantly restored sixteenth-century shops, and farther south on the east side of Cornmarket Street is the picturesque courtyard of THE GOLDEN CROSS, which has been an inn since *c.* 1200 (though since 1970 it has provided food and drink, but not accommodation). The gate is fifteenth-century and so is the north range: the half-timbered gabled south range is seventeenth-century. The six oriel windows of the north range are original.

A little nearer Carfax, on the same side of the road, at No. 3, is a fifteenth-century house, refaced in the eighteenth century, and containing, on the second floor, the PAINTED ROOM. It is so called because of the sixteenth-century designs on its plastered walls, discovered during repairs in 1927. Surviving black-letter inscriptions read: '. . . And last of this rest, be thou God's servante for that I hold best. In the Mornynge earlye serve God devoutlye . . . feare God above all thynge.' This room is of special interest, for it is almost certainly the room in which Shakespeare slept when he was the guest of the Davenants on his many journeys between Stratford and London. The Davenants owned the inn, then called 'The Crown' and Shakespeare was god-father to their son, William, later a member of Lincoln College. No. 3 Cornmarket is now the office of the Oxford Preservation Trust.

Returning northwards along Cornmarket Street we pass little of architectural interest, especially since Woolworth's has successively displaced two ancient hotels, the Roebuck (now rebuilt in Market Street) and the Clarendon (formerly the Star). A hundred yards or so down George Street (to the left of the north end of Cornmarket Street) is the NEW THEATRE, which was rebuilt in 1933. If we continue north-wards from Cornmarket Street we pass St. Mary Magda-len's Church on our right, and, continuing along St. Giles' past the Taylorian, we come first to BLACKFRIARS, built in 1921, an attractive low structure, with fine modern chapel in Perpendicular Gothic. Here members of the Dominican Order undergo four years' training for the priesthood or study for research degrees in the University.

PUSEY HOUSE is next door. It commemorates Edward Bou-verie Pusey, Canon of Christ Church and Regius Professor of Hebrew, who fought an unending battle against the rising latitudinarianism and secularism of his day. He tried hard to keep the University a preserve of the Church of England. The House, built in 1884, boasts a fine theological library and a magnificent chapel where the services are in the High Anglican tradition.

Just round the corner, in Pusey Street, is

REGENT'S PARK COLLEGE

Present strength: The Principal; 3 tutors; 42 members receiving tuition or supervision.

 REGENT'S PARK should not be called a college because it is not one, but has been a Permanent Private Hall of the University since 1957. It began in London in 1810 as a theological seminary for the Baptist ministry, but was moved to Oxford in 1940. The buildings are good and were completed in 1968 by the building of the south wing which includes a chapel on the first floor. There are a fine lecture hall and a library rich in Nonconformist literature of the seventeenth and eighteenth centuries. Some old houses in St. Giles' are incorporated in the College and the small quadrangle boasts the unique feature of a stone screen in the classical manner, shutting off the Principal's Lodging.

A little farther north we come to

ST. BENET'S HALL

Founded 1897. *Present strength*: The Master; 27 members receiving tuition or supervision.

 ST. BENET'S HALL is the community from which monks coming up from Ampleforth Abbey matriculate. A few laymen are admitted, but for the most part members are Benedictine monks. It occupies two tall houses built in 1837. Founded in 1897 St. Benet's became a Permanent Private Hall of the University in 1918.

Opposite St. Benet's Hall is Black Hall, recently refaced but dating from about 1600, and much altered 100 years later. It and the eighteenth-century house next door to the south are the home of QUEEN ELIZABETH HOUSE, established in 1954 and maintained jointly by the University and H.M. Government as a centre for the study of Commonwealth problems. Sir Ernest Oppenheimer contributed £100,000 towards this project.

A little farther south is No. 16 St. Giles', a mansion built in 1702 belonging to St. John's and until recently used by H.M. Judges of the High Court when visiting Oxford for the Assizes.

The church in the angle of the Woodstock and Banbury Roads is ST. GILES'. Its nave is twelfth-century, its tower, chancel, and aisles, early-thirteenth-century. The south chapel was added a little later and rebuilt *c.* 1850. There are eight bells.

To the west of the churchyard, through the unobtrusive entrance to Little Clarendon Street, may be seen the first stages of what will ultimately be a vast complex of University offices and departments (architect, Sir Leslie Martin).

Going north along the Woodstock Road we come next to St. Aloysius', the Roman Catholic church built in 1875, and then to

SOMERVILLE COLLEGE

Founded 1879. *Present strength*: The Principal; 21 Fellows; 1 Visiting Fellow; 12 tutors and lecturers; 17 Research Fellows; 72 scholars and exhibitioners; 320 other members receiving tuition or supervision.

 ARISING out of a movement for the higher education of women and a desire that women should be able to share some of the advantages Oxford had to offer in its teaching and examinations two colleges or, rather, halls were established in 1878–9. The first was Lady Margaret Hall, expressly for members of the Church of England, and the other was Somerville, which was to be undenominational. Both began shakily in private houses, L.M.H. with nine students, and Somerville with twelve, but they inevitably grew in size and reputation and, with the movement towards the emancipation of women and the equality of the sexes, it was only a matter of time before women were admitted, not only to the examinations, but also to the degrees of the University. In this matter Oxford led Cambridge and women were admitted to full membership in 1920.[1] Somerville was incorporated by Royal Charter in 1926 and is now entirely self-governing. It took its name and arms from Mary Somerville, 1780–1872, a brilliant mathematician, wife of William Somerville, F.R.S.

The first quadrangle we come to was the last to be built, 1933. It was designed in the style of about 1690 by Morley Horder and built in hammer-dressed Bladon stone. It has two stories with dormers and a pedimented gable in the north side. It should wear well.

Through the arch westwards we come to another quadrangle open to the south, but with the view blocked by the factory-like wall of St. Aloysius' (R.C.) Church. Here is Walton House, a fine Queen Anne mansion, the nucleus of the college. Continuous extensions have been built east and west, and southwards is Maitland, which includes the fine panelled hall on the first floor, one of the most handsome rooms in Oxford. It contains numerous fine portraits.

Through the third arch we come to the third or Garden quadrangle. The buildings are all in red-brick, in variations of the style of Queen Anne, except the chapel, 1935, which is in stone and was designed by Courtenay Theobald. It has not yet acquired any sort of venerability, but its oak stalls in a restrained Jacobean style, with a continuous bold canopy and pendent balls, are impressive. The shallow chancel is bare and unadorned as, perhaps, befits an undenominational place of worship. There is an organ gallery at the west end, but no pulpit. The dedication is 'to Jesus Christ, the Lord and Giver of Life'.

The Margery Fry and Elizabeth Nuffield House for graduates was opened in October 1964, and the Wolfson Building in 1967.

Well-known members: Dame Emily Penrose; Grace Hadow; Helen Darbishire; Lilian Mary Faithfull; Rose Macaulay; Eleanor Rathbone; Margery Fry; Winifred Holtby; Dorothy Sayers; Vera Brittain; Helen Waddell; Margaret Kennedy (Lady Davis), Barbara Ward (Lady Jackson); Lady Meynell; Dorothy Hodgkin, O.M.; Iris Murdoch.

[1] It is only fair to say that Girton College began at Hitchin in 1869 and moved to Cambridge in 1873. Newnham was founded in 1871.

41. Keble Triangle

42. University Museum

43. Rhodes House

Next door to Somerville is the RADCLIFFE INFIRMARY, built, like the Camera and the Observatory, by Dr. John Radcliffe's trustees. It was opened in 1770. The original building, by Henry Keene, is a typically handsome classical block, but it has been subjected to extensions, mostly disfiguring ones, on all sides. The Oxford University Medical School is of high repute and 'the Radcliffe' is only one of a large group of hospitals which includes the Nuffield Orthopaedic Centre, the Churchill, the Warneford, the Slade, and Littlemore. Lord Nuffield was a munificent benefactor, not least in the endowment of Chairs in Surgery, Clinical Medicine, Anaesthetics, Obstetrics, and Orthopaedic Surgery. There are fourteen professorial chairs in the Faculty of Medicine.

Adjoining the Infirmary is the RADCLIFFE OBSERVATORY (architects, Henry Keene and James Wyatt), one of the most lovely buildings in Oxford and which could be seen to better advantage when its extended wings were spread in open fields. Its date is 1772–5. The south front is 175 ft. long, each of the wings being 69 ft., and from its centre rises an octagonal tower four stages high modelled on the Tower of the Winds at Athens; the first example of Greek revival in Oxford. The wings are one-storied and the centre-piece has two stories with a balustraded platform round the tower, which is surmounted by a wind-gauge and globe, supported by the figures of Hercules and Atlas. On the north front the centre-piece protrudes in a great semicircular bay. At the east end of the east wing is the house built for the Savilian Professor of Astronomy.

On the other side of the road is

ST. ANNE'S COLLEGE

Founded, as the Society of Oxford Home Students, 1879; incorporated as St. Anne's College, 1952. *Present strength*: The Principal; 21 Fellows; 3 Research Fellows; 6 lecturers; 25 scholars; 28 exhibitioners; 373 other members receiving tuition or supervision.

 As its former name indicates, St. Anne's began as a society for women students who were living at home or with relations, but as time went on a number of houses were bought and served as hostels. Some of these were in the Banbury Road and gradually a large and compact area from Bevington Road southward was acquired. This is a splendid site and the first college building, Hartland House, appeared upon it in the mid-1930's, with an extension added in 1951 (Sir Giles Gilbert Scott). The building runs east and west and includes a fine library and common rooms. Built in the pleasant Bladon stone with Clipsham dressings, the south front is distinguished by its large steel-framed rectangular windows. What appear as flat-faced, three-storied towers are carried right back through the building to appear as twin rounded bastions with long narrow windows on the north side.

A new dining-hall to seat 300 was built in 1959 alongside the Woodstock Road. It is steel-framed, but stone-faced. Kitchens run along its west side and there is a veranda to the east. On the top is a mushroom cupola. The south end has a shallow curve and two stories to include a small dining-room and Senior Common Room: an exciting and original addition to the Oxford scene: the architect was Gerald Banks. Plans have been drawn up by Messrs. Howell, Killick & Partridge for the building of six new blocks of rooms and a tower of eleven stories. Two of the blocks are now in being and look well in their garden setting, the Rayne Building, 1968, Wolfson, 1964.

Well-known members: Elizabeth Jennings; Ivy Williams; Naomi Mitchison; Norah Lillian Preston, Principal of Bedford College, London; Margaret Irwin; Dorothy Garrod.

Immediately to the north is

ST. ANTONY'S COLLEGE

Founded 1948; opened 1950. *Present strength*: The Warden; 41 Fellows;
1 visiting Fellow; 100 other members receiving tuition or supervision.

IN September 1948 Congregation was un-
expectedly called together to hear of the
offer of a wealthy French merchant, Mon-
sieur Antonin Besse, to give the University
£1,500,000; £250,000 of this was to be given
to the less well-endowed colleges and the rest
to be used for the foundation of a new college.
In each case the benefiting colleges were to set aside a few
places or scholarships for young Frenchmen.

Exeter, Lincoln, Wadham, Pembroke, Worcester, and
Keble Colleges and St. Edmund and St. Peter's Halls (the
last became a college in 1961) shared the quarter-million—
the new college was St. Antony's. After some difficulty
a site and building were found which had until recently
been occupied by an Anglican convent. It was on an island
site, almost the whole of which has now been acquired by
the College. Plans for buildings of great interest have been
drawn up by Messrs. Howell, Killick, Partridge, and Amis,
but the means to put them into execution have so far been
lacking except that a dining hall for 200 with a suite of
ancillary rooms has been completed and brought into use
in 1971. Concrete can never have been used with more
grace and acceptability: it is a building as attractive as it is
imaginative and original.

The old Convent building meanwhile houses in the
former chapel and elsewhere the library which includes
a unique Russian collection of 25,000 volumes and owes a
great deal to the generosity of the Gulbenkian Foundation.

At present the College is postgraduate and the work is
largely research in modern history and politics, British,
European, and international.

Just beyond the church of St. Philip and St. James we
come to another large rectangular site and this is occupied by

ST. HUGH'S COLLEGE

Founded 1886. *Present strength*: The Principal; 25 Fellows; 10 lecturers; 5 Research Fellows; 2 Rawnsley Students; 2 senior scholars; 34 scholars; 35 exhibitioners; 334 other members receiving tuition or supervision.

 ST. HUGH'S began humbly in a semi-detached house in Norham Road as a hostel for poor students who could not afford the charges at Lady Margaret Hall. It was founded (1886) by Elizabeth Wordsworth, then Principal of L.M.H., whose father had been Bishop of Lincoln and the Hall was named after the greatest occupant of that see, the thirteenth-century St. Hugh. In 1888 the Hall moved to Norham Gardens and thence in 1916, to its present site. It was incorporated by Royal Charter in 1926.

The main entrance is under a cupola in St. Margaret's Road and the buildings are a long range running east and west with prongs jutting south into the lovely garden. The hall, at the east end, was extended in 1958. The fine library, named after the first Principal, Miss C. A. E. Moberly, is towards the west. The chapel is a room over the main entrance. All these buildings are in early eighteenth-century style, the architect being H. T. Buckland. But the additions made during the nineteen-sixties are in the style of their own time, executed in a peculiarly harsh red brick.

Well-known members: Annie M. A. H. Rogers; C. M. Ady; Joan Evans; Margaret Lane, Countess of Huntingdon; Mary Cartwright, F.R.S., Mistress of Girton; Mary Renault; Barbara Castle, M.P.

Returning towards Oxford along the Banbury Road past Park Town, a delightful example of town-planning dating from *c*. 1858, with the famous Dragon School behind it to the east, we come to Norham Road which takes us past the Maison Française on our left.

The MAISON FRANÇAISE came into being in 1946 inspired by the will to cement Anglo-French friendship and to revive the close relationship which prevailed between the Universities of Paris and Oxford in the Middle Ages.

Backed by the Sorbonne and the French government, the Maison was for over twenty years at 72 Woodstock Road, serving as 'a cultural centre and a mini-residential college'.

In its new specially designed quarters, with reception, dining, and visiting facilities, its library of over 21,000 volumes and its innumerable French papers and periodicals and journals, its auditorium and common rooms, it is a veritable France in Oxford.

Continuing eastwards we come to Fyfield Road on our right, which leads into Norham Gardens; on the left is the main entrance to

LADY MARGARET HALL

Founded 1878. *Present strength*: The Principal; 26 Fellows; a chaplain; 5 Research Fellows; 9 lecturers; 42 scholars; 17 exhibitioners; 362 other members receiving tuition or supervision.

THE emergence of L.M.H. and Somerville has already been described (see p. 125). It was accomplished despite the steady opposition of those who thought Oxford a most unsuitable place for the education of women and of those who thought women to be unsuited for education. The chief driving force was provided by Dr. E. S. Talbot, then Warden of Keble and later Bishop of Winchester.

A house was found at the end of Norham Gardens and backing on to the Parks. The first Principal (1878), Elizabeth Wordsworth, daughter of the Bishop of Lincoln, presided over nine young ladies and at her suggestion the Hall was called after Henry VII's mother, the Lady Margaret Beaufort, who had founded Christ's and St. John's Colleges at Cambridge and the Lady Margaret Professorships of Divinity at both the Universities.

The Hall soon outgrew the 'white house' and extensions were built in 1881 and 1883. These were built by Basil Champneys. In 1896 a larger block named after Miss Wordsworth was opened. This was designed by Sir Reginald

Blomfield, an expert in French Renaissance architecture and he subsequently built Talbot, 1909, containing hall and library, and Toynbee, 1915. In 1926 he built Lodge, a block which joins Wordsworth to the original buildings.

L.M.H. has always commanded the allegiance of vivid personalities and one of these, Miss Margaret Deneke, was carrying out a musical tour in America in order to raise funds for the Hall, when Mrs. Edward S. Harkness gave £35,000 for the erection of yet another block to be called after Miss Deneke. This was finished in 1932 to the designs of Sir Giles Gilbert Scott, who also built the chapel in Byzantine style just to the north of it, at the same time. It was dedicated in 1933 by the venerable Founder, Dr. Talbot.

The Lynda Grier Library (architect, Raymond Erith) was finished in 1961, running east and west in line with Toynbee, making the third side of a quadrangle of which Talbot on the east and Lodge on the south are the other two sides. The Library has 50,000 books and room for seventy readers. In 1965-6 with the aid of a munificent grant from the Wolfson Foundation, the quadrangle was completed with the buildings known as Wolfson West and North (R. Erith).

Two more residential blocks are being built along the east side of Fyfield Road (architect, Christophe Grillet) and should be completed in 1972.

The College has spacious and beautiful gardens running down to the Cherwell.

Like the other women's colleges, L.M.H. is building up a good collection of portraits and these, together with the panelling in the former dining-hall in Talbot and the stalls in the chapel are worth seeing.

Well-known members: Dame Elizabeth Wordsworth; Eleanor F. Jourdain; Eleanor C. Lodge; Gertrude Lowthian Bell; Mrs. Barbara Hammond; Agnes Maude Royden; Viscountess Rhondda; Dame Veronica Wedgwood; H. F. M. Prescott; Margaret Rawlings; Dame Mary Smieton; Lady Pakenham; H.R.H. Princess Astrid of Norway.

On leaving L.M.H. we may go down Norham Gardens, passing St. Stephen's House, an Anglican theological college, the Department of Education, and Wycliffe Hall, also a Church of England theological college generally evangelical in character. On our left is the main entrance to the Parks, as the University Park is generally called; it was here that Charles I's artillery was parked in 1642. Here we find ourselves in a wide acreage, bounded on the east by the River Cherwell. There are fine trees, the University Cricket Ground—the only place in England where first-class cricket may be seen free of charge—lawn-tennis courts and hockey pitches, two croquet lawns, and away in the south-east corner PARSON'S PLEASURE, a famous bathing-place for men where no swimming clothes are needed. Just beyond it one can either pass through a gate on the right and follow the riverbank to Magdalen College, or go straight on between the river and a mill-race along the path known as MESO-POTAMIA; it emerges by the Magdalen cricket ground in Marston Road.

The watermeadows on the left bank of the river were given to the University by Mr. and Mrs. Henry Spalding in 1944 as a memorial to Dudley Buxton: the 'Rainbow Bridge' was built in 1927. It has the remarkable attributes of appearing beautiful to those who see it and of remaining invisible, hidden by the trees, to those who would rather not see it: a great success from whatever direction it is approached, but not recommended for those pushing heavy prams.

There are numerous exits from the Parks. Those to the south take us to the region of the laboratories, to the New College, Merton, and Balliol playing-fields, Holywell Manor, St. Cross Church; that to the north, to Norham Gardens, and Lady Margaret Hall. Those to the west take us to the area bounded by Banbury, Parks, and Keble Roads. This is known as the Keble Road Triangle and is being developed with a co-ordinated plan as an extension of the older Science Area which is in the south-western corner of the Parks. The massive nine-storey block which dominates the Triangle is

The ENGINEERING LABORATORY (Ramsey, Murray, White, and Ward) which was opened in 1963, replacing a cramped and inadequate building at the northern apex of the Triangle in which Engineering had been taught since 1914.

The new building provides facilities for an annual intake of over 140 undergraduates as well as for research. A joint School of Engineering and Economics has recently been established. The DEPARTMENT OF METALLURGY on the eastern side of the Triangle overlooking the Parks was completed in 1959 and is already being extended. Among its research equipment is one of the most powerful electron microscopes in the world, used to study the structures of metals and alloys. Both Engineering and Metallurgy are expanding undergraduate subjects. At the junction of Keble and Banbury Roads is the NUCLEAR PHYSICS LABORATORY (Ove Arup, 1970). The striking building composed of an upright fan-shaped assembly of tall concrete beams houses a Van der Graaf generator which enables ions to be accelerated to energies exceeding 20 million volts for the study of the structure of the atomic nucleus. Much of the experimental work by members of the laboratory is carried out using the large accelerators at Harwell or at the joint European laboratory near Geneva, the results being processed and analysed at Oxford. A few yards to the south, at the beginning of St. Giles' is the MATHEMATICAL INSTITUTE which provides lecture rooms, offices for members of the academic staff, library and common-room facilities, and the faculty headquarters for the subject.

The Victorian terrace on the north side of Keble Road, which will eventually be replaced by further new buildings, provides temporary accommodation for a variety of scientific and other departments until more permanent accommodation is found for them. Notable among these is the LABORATORY FOR RESEARCH IN ARCHAEOLOGY which is distinguished for the devising of instruments for surveying archaeological sites, both on land and under water, and for methods of dating ceramics. Tests in this laboratory have recently detected considerable numbers of fake antiquities in museums and other collections.

We now come to

44. Zoology Building

45. Law Library

46. St. Catherine's

47. Mansfield College.

KEBLE COLLEGE

Founded 1870. *Present strength*: The Warden; 34 Fellows; 1 Research Fellow; 7 lecturers; 5 senior scholars; 63 scholars; 51 exhibitioners; 297 other members receiving tuition or supervision.

 WHEN John Keble died in 1866 his admirers invited subscriptions for a new college to be run on economical lines and thus enable men to come up to Oxford who could not otherwise afford it. Naturally it was to be closely associated with that branch of the Church of England to which Keble had devoted his life, but the college is open to men of all beliefs or of none, though some of the scholarships are restricted to members of the Anglican Church.

The College was opened in 1870 and next year was admitted to the status of a 'New Foundation'. This meant that it was not, like the other colleges, self-governing, but had a Council, consisting of eminent members of the University, mostly non-resident, who exercised a general supervision, the Warden being responsible for the internal administration. As the years went by the College assumed the usual pattern, the tutors became Fellows and the powers of the Council faded away. In 1952 it became entirely self-governing, constitutionally the equal of the others, though, like the women's colleges, it lacks substantial endowment.

Two things at once differentiate Keble from other men's colleges. It was built in red-brick, diversified with stone dressings and yellow and blue bricks in patterns; and instead of the traditional staircase arrangement, undergraduates' rooms were strung out along corridors on each floor, as in the women's colleges.

The architect was William Butterfield and the buildings are a bold and unique contribution to the Oxford scene. The design is uniform and consistent, but the chapel, given by William Gibbs, dominates the whole. It is of cathedral proportions and, mellowing well, is most impressive from the Parks. The interior is remarkable for its coloured mosaics, Gothic arcading, and vaulted roof. In a small side-chapel, added in 1892, can be seen Holman Hunt's famous picture, *The Light of the World*. The vast and lofty hall and library were finished in 1878, the gift of Antony and Martin Gibbs, sons of the donor of the chapel. The completion of the north side of the College was made possible in 1957 as a result of the Besse benefaction (see p. 129).

To mark the centenary of the College in 1970 an appeal for money was issued with a view to building a new quadrangle to the west of the Warden's lodgings, and along Museum and Blackhall Roads. Messrs. Ahrends, Burton, and Koralek are the architects of what promises to be an admirable addition to the College, boldly different, but all to scale.

Famous men: A. F. Winnington-Ingram, Bishop of London; D. L. Prosser, Archbishop of Wales; C. F. Garbett, Archbishop of York. The College has contributed an outstanding number of the leaders of the Church of England during the last eighty years.

THE SCIENCE AREA

THERE have been three outstanding periods in the history of Science in Oxford. The first was in the thirteenth and fourteenth centuries and was illuminated by the genius of Robert Grosseteste, Roger Bacon, and Thomas Bradwardine. The second came in the seventeenth century when William Harvey, a Cambridge man who discovered the circulation of the blood, was Warden of Merton; when Thomas Sydenham, the great physician, was a Fellow of All Souls; and when the meetings out of which the Royal Society began were held in the Lodgings of Warden Wilkins at Wadham. The great names in this group were those of Wren, Seth Ward, Robert Boyle, Robert Hooke, Ralph Bathurst, and John Mayow. Hard upon their heels came Edmund Halley and James Bradley, the astronomers. The third period began in the middle of the nineteenth century with the establishment of the Honours School of Natural Science in 1850 (two years later than the Natural Sciences Tripos at Cambridge). The study of science has expanded ever since until it now includes over 40 per cent of the Oxford student body. The scientific departments and laboratories are therefore of the greatest importance in the academic life of Oxford. They are concentrated here in the Science Area in the south-western and southern parts of the University Parks, and, as we have already seen, are expanding into the Keble Road Triangle. The first building in the Parks nearly opposite Keble was

THE UNIVERSITY MUSEUM built in 1855 in the heyday of Victorian optimism, expansion, and achievement. It originated in a recommendation of the Commissioners of 1850-2 who wanted to see the professorial system restored as a supplement to the teaching provided by the colleges and who felt that science was in a special sense a task for the University rather than for the individual colleges. Central to the idea was the building of a museum, not only to house all the University's scattered scientific collections but also to provide facilities for professorial instruction, lecture rooms, and laboratories.

The driving force was supplied by Henry Acland, soon to become Regius Professor of Medicine (1858-94), and his friend John Ruskin, both of Christ Church, and the material result was the great pile of Venetian Gothic in front of us. Old prints suggest that it looked better in spacious isolation than it does now, closely flanked by the Radcliffe Science Library and the Inorganic Chemistry Laboratory to the south and the Department of Geology to the north. Justice demands that it should have the waters of the Grand Canal in front of it and its own reflection as a foil: the lawns which were in front of it for the first 120 years were not enough, and the great excavations for the sinking of an underground extension of the Radcliffe Library under these lawns make one apprehensive for the future. Be that as it may, it represented a new departure. It is a monument to great enthusiasm in the face of strong conservative opposition and was accomplished on restricted resources: that is why some pillars and capitals are carved and some not.

There is a long west front with north and south wings enclosing a great glass-covered and galleried court. Jutting out to the south was an independent Chemistry Laboratory built on the plan of the Abbot's Kitchen at Glastonbury: it was a fixed notion of Ruskin's that Gothic was best for all purposes. The main building provided laboratories and lecture and exhibition rooms for Medicine, Experimental Philosophy (Physics), Mineralogy, Geology, Anatomy, Physiology, and Zoology. The Hope Department of Entomology has grown out of the collection of insects and crustacea given by the Rev. F. W. Hope in 1849. The exhibited collections are designed for student instruction in the fields of zoology, geology, and mineralogy, rather than for popular display. Notable among the exhibits in the central court are the head and foot, all that remain, of a specimen of the extinct dodo of Mauritius that was in the Tradescant collection; enormous bones of *Ceteosaurus oxoniensis*, a creature that lived 150 million years ago and specimens of minerals and precious stones.

Behind the central court is the PITT RIVERS MUSEUM OF ETHNOLOGY AND PRE-HISTORY, the nucleus of which was given to the University in 1885 by General A. H. Lane Fox Pitt-Rivers. It includes items collected by the celebrated Captain Cook (1728–79) and other explorers of the eighteenth and nineteenth centuries, and a mass of fascinating anthropological material.

As scientific studies and research rapidly expanded, the quarters provided in the Museum soon became inadequate. New laboratories grew up behind the Museum and the Science Area expanded steadily eastward. During much of this expansion space and money were short; as a result the older parts of the area consist of buildings tightly packed together, often repeatedly modified and enlarged, in a variety of styles or in no style.

The RADCLIFFE SCIENCE LIBRARY (1901; T. G. Jackson. New wing 1934; Sir Hubert Worthington. New underground extension under construction) at the corner of Parks and South Parks Road, is effectively the scientific section of the Bodleian Library. It caters for all the scientific faculties in the University. Many of the individual laboratories have their own specialized research libraries, some of them large and important.

To the north of the University Museum is

The DEPARTMENT OF GEOLOGY AND MINERALOGY which was enlarged and modernized in 1949 (Lanchester and Lodge). Inside the stone façade the building retains much of the Victorian Gothic brickwork of the original Clarendon physics laboratory built in 1868 on this site. The department is particularly noted for geochemical work, especially the determination of the age of rocks (such as those from the moon) by isotope ratio measurements using mass spectrometry. To the north is

The CLARENDON LABORATORY (Physics). The present main building dates from 1940; the adjacent Townsend Electrical Laboratory was the gift of the Drapers' Company in 1910. The Clarendon at Oxford corresponds to the Cavendish at Cambridge and after the First World War was developed enormously by the late Professor Lindemann, who became Lord Cherwell, and was Sir Winston Churchill's chief scientific adviser during the Second World War. It is distinguished for its work at very low temperatures and with very high magnetic fields, as well as for work in many other branches of physics. The departments of Nuclear and Theoretical physics in the Keble Road Triangle form part of the physics department and together with the Clarendon provide for nearly 200 research workers and 300 undergraduates. An internal road starts by the Clarendon Laboratory and winds its way through the Science Area to join South Parks Road. To the north of this road, running along the southern side of the Parks is

The DEPARTMENT OF PHYSIOLOGY (Lanchester and Lodge, 1953). At Oxford those intending to study medicine begin by taking an Honours B.A. degree in Physiology, working in this department. At the same time they study the so-called pre-clinical subjects of anatomy and biochemistry, followed later by pathology, bacteriology, and pharmacology, after which they embark on their clinical training, either at the Radcliffe Hospital in Oxford or elsewhere.

The DEPARTMENT OF BIOCHEMISTRY was originally established in 1924 with the help of a benefaction from the Rockefeller Foundation. The extension completed in 1963 is the highest and most conspicuous building in the area. In addition to those reading the Honours School of Biochemistry the department provides instruction for those reading medicine as does

The DEPARTMENT OF HUMAN ANATOMY, originally built behind the Museum in 1892 and several times extended. Research in this department is much concerned with the nervous system and elaborate equipment for this work includes several electron microscopes.

Opposite the Radcliffe Science Library in South Parks Road is

RHODES HOUSE (architect, Sir Herbert Barker), domed and porticoed somewhat fussily but handsome none the less and expensively built in 1929 on land bought from Wadham. It provides a centre for the study of the social, political, and economic history of the British Commonwealth, the United States, and Africa and it houses the Bodleian books in these fields published since 1760. There is a fine hall and the whole building is distinguished by very high quality workmanship, especially of the woodwork. The circular entrance foyer contains memorials to Rhodes Scholars who died in the two wars, including those from Germany.

Over much of its length South Parks Road is attractively lined with lime trees—a reminder that within living memory this was the southern boundary of the Parks. Many of the buildings here are chemistry laboratories. This is an important subject in Oxford, involving almost ten per cent of the entire university population—by far the largest chemistry school in the country.

Next to the Radcliffe Library and opposite Rhodes House is the INORGANIC CHEMISTRY LABORATORY. The rather heavy stone façade of the extensions added in 1957 was not a very successful attempt to maintain a consistent style for the buildings along this section of South Parks Road. Parts of the inside of the building date back to the middle of the nineteenth century; the main undergraduate teaching laboratory was built in 1876. The building also accommodates the Department of Chemical Crystallography; it was for work done here on the structure of vitamin B_{12} by X-ray crystal analysis that Professor Dorothy Hodgkin received the Nobel Prize in 1964. The next building is

The DEPARTMENT OF CHEMICAL PHARMACOLOGY, greatly enlarged in 1961 by a curtain-wall extension faced in brown glass (Gollins, Melvin, Ward, and Partners). In addition to the provision of instruction in pharmacology for medical students, physiologists, and chemists the laboratory carries out research into the chemical mechanism for drug action and the transmission of activity in nerves, using chemical, biochemical, and physiological methods.

The organic chemistry department is known as

The DYSON PERRINS LABORATORY, funds for the original building constructed in 1916 having been provided by Mr. Dyson Perrins. The laboratory has been many times enlarged, especially in 1960 when a new wing and a modern lecture theatre were added (Ramsey, Murray, White, and Ward). At this point the internal road running through the Science Area joins South Parks Road. It is lined with particularly fine flowering cherry trees which make a marvellous show at Easter time. On the east of this road is

The PHYSICAL CHEMISTRY LABORATORY (Lanchester and Lodge) given to the University by Lord Nuffield and opened in 1941. Previously research and teaching in physical chemistry had been conducted in somewhat makeshift laboratories—many of them in cellars—provided by Balliol and Trinity, and this contribution by the colleges is acknowledged by their coats of arms on the new building. In 1966 two new floors were added, increasing the available space by 40 per cent, without destroying the appearance of the building—indeed it is not obvious that the building has been extended in this way, an advantage perhaps of a conventional brick structure and of having the original architects design the extension.

On the edge of the Parks the white domes of the University Observatory can be seen, now housing

The DEPARTMENT OF ASTROPHYSICS, which is primarily concerned with solar studies. The domes do not contain conventional telescopes; they cover systems of mirrors which direct light from the sun down to very large spectro-graphs located in the basement.

Next to the Physical Chemistry Laboratory is

The DEPARTMENT OF FORESTRY (Sir Hubert Worthing-ton, 1950), which houses both the Commonwealth Forestry Institute and the University Forestry School. Generous donations towards the cost of this building were made by the Rajah of Sarawak, the Rhodes Trustees, and the Pilgrim Trust. The building is remarkable for some fine woodwork and panelling in interesting and unusual woods the timber for which was presented by Dominion and Colonial govern-ments; also for its 'library' of 25,000 specimens of wood. The department makes use of Bagley Wood, which belongs to St. John's and lies on the road to Abingdon, and the Wytham estate to the west of Oxford, which belongs to the University, for experimental work and demonstration plots, a total area of 1,400 acres.

The DEPARTMENT OF BOTANY, behind Forestry, contains an important library and very large herbarium collections including that of Claridge Druce, an Oxford apothecary and student of British flora. The Botanic Garden remains near Magdalen Bridge and there is a small genetic garden near the Observatory on the edge of the Parks.

At the end of the South Parks Road is

The PATHOLOGY DEPARTMENT, given to the University by the trustees of Sir William Dunn. The attractive brick building (E. Warren, 1927) is set back from the road behind a screen of trees. An animal house and new extensions largely financed by the Wellcome Foundation are at the rear. The laboratory teaches pathology and bacteriology to medical students. It was here during the Second World War that a team under Sir Howard Florey first produced penicillin and carried out the initial clinical trials. Here the road turns south and becomes St. Cross Road, on the other side of which stands

The ZOOLOGY LABORATORY (Sir Leslie Martin, 1970), sited on what was previously the Merton playing field, generously made available to the University by the College after Congregation had rejected proposals to make a further encroachment into the Parks and build the laboratory there in the form of a very high tower block. The laboratory with its lavish equipment and spacious circulation areas makes a striking contrast with the elderly and crowded accommodation of much of the physical sciences. The building also accommodates the Laboratory of Molecular Biophysics. A large lecture theatre is shared with

The DEPARTMENT OF EXPERIMENTAL PSYCHOLOGY which adjoins it. This department provides teaching for the Honours School of Psychology, Philosophy, and Physiology (P.P.P.) as well as for research with both human and animal subjects.

At the corner of the road is an entrance to the University Parks and a path leading to the Parson's Pleasure bathing place and to Mesopotamia.

St. Cross Road, to the right, leads to the Church of ST. CROSS, Holywell, which now serves as the chapel of St. Catherine's. Its chancel is twelfth-century Norman, c. 1100, and its squat tower is thirteenth century. Adjoining the church to the north is the picturesque HOLYWELL MANOR, formerly belonging to Merton College and rebuilt in 1516. In 1925 it was enlarged and adapted by Balliol for extra accommodation but from 1967 it has been used, together with Sir Leslie Martin's 'Holywell Minor' opposite, as a graduate centre for its own men and St. Anne's women— 57 men and 24 women, some of each in each.

From here we may see as we turn down Manor Road the BODLEIAN LAW LIBRARY, with which are combined in the same group, the INSTITUTE OF STATISTICS and the ENGLISH FACULTY LIBRARY (Sir Leslie Martin, 1964). Each of these departments is distinct from the rest, with its own reading, seminar, and other rooms. There is space for 450,000 books and 320 readers in the Law Library: the English Library has 80,000 volumes and seats for 150 readers. The Institute of Statistics has only 50,000 books.

At the end of Manor Road is

ST. CATHERINE'S COLLEGE

Founded 1962. *Present strength*: The Master; 37 Fellows; 2 Supernumerary Fellows; 10 lecturers; 61 scholars; 7 honorary scholars; 51 exhibitioners; 401 other members receiving tuition or supervision.

 WHEN the status of Servitor was abolished together with that of Nobleman in 1850 it became difficult for poor men to get into the University and so, in 1868, a society was founded to matriculate men not belonging to any college or hall but subject to the discipline of the Delegacy of Non-Collegiate Students. From 1930 this society used the name of St. Catherine's, derived from an earlier club room which was incorrectly believed to stand on the site of St. Catherine's Chapel. The first headquarters of the society were in the Old Clarendon Building, but in 1888 a move was made to more commodious premises adjoining the new Examination Schools in High Street. They were in their turn also outgrown and in 1936 a further move was made to the buildings in St. Aldate's which now belong to Linacre College. The Society was here for twenty-six years. It admitted not only undergraduates, but many graduates of other universities who wanted an Oxford degree.

The most famous member of the old St. Catherine's was H. H. Henson, Bishop of Durham, who took a First in History in 1884, and was elected a Fellow of All Souls the same year.

The new St. Catherine's, like Churchill College at Cambridge, is a product of the technological age which has followed the Second World War, and the accent is on science, but, since it is in Oxford, it has been ruled that half its members shall be Arts men so as to ensure that liberal education so much prized by the Oxonian.

The College had no single founder, though it would hardly have come into existence without the impetus and wisdom of its present Master Sir Alan Bullock. Most of the money came from the great educational foundations and from leading firms in industry and commerce, but the largest single donation came from a St. Catherine's man, Dr. Rudolph Light, who gave a million dollars.

A site was found in Holywell Great Meadow between two arms of the River Cherwell. The architect was the Dane, Arne Jacobsen, who brought to the special problems arising in a twentieth-century college a mind not unsympathetic or insensitive to the Oxford scene, but unfettered by the Oxford tradition.

The result is not something that has grown, but something that has been put: it is a striking piece of geometry, a great rectangle, containing rectangles, with here and there a circle, symmetrical, well balanced, in a large frame of grass and trees. All is vertical or horizontal and flat except the leaf-like curls of the furniture, formal but not pompous, economical without meanness.

The dining hall, given by Esso Petroleum, is the largest in either Oxford or Cambridge. The Wolfson Foundation gave the library with room for 100,000 volumes, and the Bernard Sunley Trust gave a magnificent lecture theatre, with Graduate Common Room and seminar rooms. The unique Music House, a low polygonal tower, stands aloof on the river bank, the gift of the Hon. Mrs. Sybil Whitamore, as a memorial to the Borthwick family. The gardens were designed by the architect and given by the Coulthurst Trust.

St. Cross Church, as we have seen (p. 143) serves as the College Chapel.

Between St. Cross Church and the wall which surrounds Magdalen Grove is the old Vicarage which is the temporary home of

ST. CROSS COLLEGE

Founded 1965. *Present strength*: The Warden; 56 Fellows; 3 Visiting Fellows; 8 graduate scholars; 2 other members receiving supervision.

AT present St. Cross can do little more than provide its fellows, most of whom hold various offices or lectureships in the University, with dinner and common rooms, and the honourable status which the fellowship of any college confers.

Opposite and at the west end of Jowett's Walk is the GEOGRAPHY SCHOOL, housed in what was a large private residence built by Dr. Mee: to this has been added a good lecture theatre designed by Sir Hubert Worthington. Opposite is MANCHESTER COLLEGE which is not yet a constituent part of the University. It began as one of the famous 'Dissenting Academies' of which there were several in the eighteenth century, when Noncomformists were subject to sundry disadvantages and, in particular, were excluded from Oxford and Cambridge. It was established at Manchester in 1786, in succession to Warrington Academy founded in 1757, moved to York in 1803, returned to Manchester in 1840, and went to London in 1853. In 1888 it came to Oxford. Though calling itself 'undenominational' most of its subscribers and members have always been Unitarian. They are a small and were formerly a wealthy body and no expense was spared in the erection of the College, which is in late Victorian Gothic (1893; T. Worthington), dressed, unfortunately, with hard and alien Derbyshire stone. The library is well stocked with books on theology and Nonconformist history. The chapel is richly panelled and has an interesting set of Burne-Jones windows. The Arlosh Hall, built in 1915, is one of the most successful of modern Oxford buildings (architect, Sir Percy Worthington) combining modest Gothic dignity with purposefulness. The College has had three famous Principals, James Martineau; Estlin Carpenter, the first Nonconformist ever to be made a D.D. by the University; and L. P. Jacks. It exists primarily to train men for the Unitarian ministry.

North of Manchester College, and also on the west side of Mansfield Road, is

MANSFIELD COLLEGE

Present strength: The Principal; 7 Fellows; 4 lecturers; 1 chaplain; 86 B.A.s and commoners.

MANSFIELD COLLEGE, built in the form of an open court facing south is generally considered to be one of the best works of Basil Champneys. Like Manchester College, it exists primarily as a theological training college for the Ministry and is supported by the Congregationalists. It began in Birmingham in 1838, but moved to Oxford in 1886 and bears the name of its principal Founders. In 1955 it became a 'Permanent Private Hall' of the University, which means that it can now present its members for matriculation by the Vice-Chancellor. As in the case of Regent's Park (p. 124) 'Hall' would be a more proper designation than 'College' and it is a pity that the change was not insisted upon.

As one faces the buildings from the lawn, the Principal's house is on the left flank and the chapel, with interesting stained glass and elaborately carved stalls, on the right. A new range of buildings on the lawn to the south was completed in 1961: the architect was Thomas Rayson.

A. M. Fairbairn, W. B. Selbie (Brasenose), and Nathaniel Micklem (New College), have been distinguished Principals.

From here we may go south down Mansfield Road to Holywell Street (p. 77), and so back to the centre of the city. Or, given plenty of time and energy, we may set off northwards in search of

WOLFSON COLLEGE

Founded 1966. *Present strength*: The President; 56 Fellows; 6 Visiting Fellows; 3 Research Fellows; 16 junior Research Fellows; 76 graduate students.

WOLFSON COLLEGE is not easily fitted into the itinerary but is nearest to St. Hugh's and Lady Margaret Hall. It may be approached from Banbury Road down Linton

Road or from Norham Road by the Dragon School lane and Chadlington Road.

The buildings should be ready for occupation by October 1972, but the College has existed as a non-residential society since 1966, with common and dining rooms in a house in Banbury Road.

Another by-product of the technological age, it is unique in that it will take 200 graduate students, men and women, married or unmarried, with or without children. Half will be resident in College. There is no restriction of subjects, but the majority will be scientists working for higher degrees. Accommodation will include flats of various sizes, a 'drug store', an underground car-park for 82 cars and space for 70 more in 'reasonably inconspicuous places'. There will be a harbour and boathouse on the river bank and a footbridge over the river to the meadows on the other side.

The site covers nine acres of water meadow. It will be the largest graduate college in Britain. The architects are Powell and Moya.

PLACES OF INTEREST
NEAR OXFORD

OWING to the ubiquity of the motor-car, which destroys
every beauty to which it gains access, the Oxford country is
not what it was. But there is still a lovely walk along the
upper river opposite Port Meadow and hereabouts the
'Trout' Inn, Godstow Nunnery, Binsey (with its holy well
and twelfth-century church), and Wytham are all worth
visiting on foot.

To the west lies the *Scholar Gypsy* country of Matthew
Arnold—Hinksey Hill, Cumnor Hurst (fine church at Cumnor), Childswell Farm, Boars Hill, and Bagley Wood.

To the east lies Shotover Hill, with a good common for
walking over.

To the north are Marston, Elsfield, Beckley, Wood
Eaton, and Islip, all with interesting churches and beautiful
houses.

Farther afield there are a great many places worth seeing,
e.g. Abingdon, Woodstock (for Blenheim Palace: seat of the
Duke of Marlborough and birthplace of Sir Winston
Churchill), Dorchester (Abbey), Witney, and Burford. For
these a guide and map of the country are recommended.

The better-known country houses in Oxfordshire include:
Rousham House (Mr. C. Cottrell-Dormer); Broughton
Castle (Lord Saye and Sele); Chastleton House (Mr. A.
Clutton Brock); Mapledurham House (Mr. J. J. Eyston);
all of which, together with Blenheim Palace, are open to
the public at stated times.

SOME BOOKS ABOUT
OXFORD

J. WELLS, *Oxford and its Colleges* (London, 1899 and later). An illustrated, scholarly pocket guide, now out of print, interestingly written.

C. E. MALLET, *A History of the University of Oxford* (3 vols., London, 1924–7).

L. H. D. BUXTON and S. GIBSON, *Oxford University Ceremonies* (Oxford, 1935).

CHRISTOPHER HOBHOUSE, *Oxford* (London, 1939; revised by Marcus Dick 1952). A brilliant historical sketch, beautifully illustrated.

HISTORICAL MONUMENTS COMMISSION, *An Inventory of the Historical Monuments in the City of Oxford* (London, 1939). Brilliantly and lavishly illustrated.

W. J. ARKELL, *Oxford Stone* (London, 1947). A short account of the kinds of stone of which Oxford is built: well illustrated.

THOMAS SHARP, *Oxford Replanned* (London, 1948). A vision of what might have been, brilliantly illustrated.

RUTH FASNACHT, *The City of Oxford* (Oxford, 1953). A good history of the city.

A. F. MARTIN and R. W. STEEL (eds.), *The Oxford Region* (Oxford, 1954). An account of the neighbourhood in many aspects compiled for the meeting of the British Association in Oxford in 1954.

M. D. LOBEL (ed.), *The Victoria History of the County of Oxford*, vol. iii: *The University of Oxford* (Oxford, 1954).

LORD HORDER, *In Praise of Oxford: an Anthology* (London, 1955). A small volume of poetry and prose.

DACRE BALSDON, *Oxford Life* (London, 1957 or later). The best modern account of undergraduate life in Oxford.

O.U. DESIGN SOCIETY, *New Oxford* (Oxford, 1961). Valuable illustrated lists of new, completed, and proposed buildings for both University and City.

W. A. PANTIN, *Oxford Life in Oxford Archives* (Oxford, 1972).

There are also many books about individual colleges and the volumes published by the Oxford Historical Society, which include *The Life and Times of Anthony Wood*, ed. by Andrew Clark (London, 1932) (now available again in the 'World's Classics' series published by the Oxford University Press).

Several colleges have on sale in the porter's lodge excellent guides to their own buildings.

INDEX

All Saints' Church, 94.
All Souls College, 58.
Archaeology, Laboratory for Research in, 134.
Ashmolean Museum, 110.

Balliol College, 99.
Blackfriars, 123.
Bodleian Law Library, 143.
Bodleian Library, 82.
Botanic Garden, 38.
Brasenose College, 64

Campion Hall, 18.
Carfax, 14.
Castle, The, 118.
Cathedral, The, 24.
Christ Church, 21.
Clarendon Building, 82.
Clarendon Physics Laboratory, 139.
Clarendon Press, 114.
Convocation House, 84.
Corpus Christi College, 30.
Cowley Fathers, 40.

DEPARTMENT OF:
  Astrophysics, 141.
  Biochemistry, 139.
  Botany, 142.
  Chemical Pharmacology, 141.
  Education, 132.
  Experimental Psychology, 143.
  Forestry, 142.
  Geology and Mineralogy, 139.
  Human Anatomy, 140.
  Metallurgy, 134.
  Pathology, 142.
  Physiology, 139.
Divinity School, 83.
'Duke Humphrey', 83.

Dyson Perrins Laboratory, 141.

Engineering Laboratory, 133.
English Faculty Library, 143.
Examination Schools, 47.
Exeter College, 88.

Folly Bridge, 19.

Geography School, 146.
Golden Cross Hotel, 122.
Greyfriars, 40.

Halifax House, 138.
Hertford College, 68.
Holywell Manor, 143.
Holywell Music Room, 77.
Hythe Bridge, 119.

Iffley Church, 20.
Information Bureau, 14-15.
Inorganic Chemistry Laboratory, 140.

Jesus College, 94.

Keble College, 135.
Keble Road Triangle, 133.
King's Arms Hotel, 76.

Lady Margaret Hall, 131.
Linacre College, 20.
Lincoln College, 91.

Magdalen College, 41.
Maison Française, 130.
Manchester College, 146.
Mansfield College, 147.
Martyrs' Memorial, 105.
Mathematical Institute, 134.

Merton College, 33.
Mesopotamia, 133.
Mitre Hotel, 94.
Music Room, 77.

New College, 71.
New Theatre, The, 123.
Nuclear Physics Laboratory, 134.
Nuffield College, 117.

Old Ashmolean Museum, 87.
Oriel College, 28.

Painted Room, The, 123.
Parks, The, 133.
Parson's Pleasure, 133.
Pembroke College, 16.
Physical Chemistry Laboratory, 141.
Physics Laboratory, The Clarendon, 139.
Pitt Rivers Museum, 138.
Playhouse, The, 110.
Pusey House, 123.

Queen Elizabeth House, 124.
Queen's College, The, 40, 52.

Radcliffe Infirmary, 127.
Radcliffe Library or Camera, 67.
Radcliffe Observatory, 127.
Radcliffe Science Library, 138.
Regent's Park College, 124.
Rhodes House, 140.
Ruskin College, 114.

St. Aldate's Church, 16.
St. Aloysius' Church, 125.
St. Anne's College, 128.
St. Antony's College, 129.
St. Barnabas' Church, 116.
St. Benet's Hall, 124.
St. Catherine's College, 144.

St. Cross Church (Holywell), 143.
St. Cross College, 143.
St. Ebbe's Church, 15.
St. Edmund Hall, 49.
St. Giles' Church, 125.
St. Hilda's College, 39.
St. Hugh's College, 130.
St. John the Evangelist Church (Cowley Fathers), 40.
St. John's College, 106.
St. Mary Magdalene's Church, 105.
St. Mary the Virgin Church (The University Church), 62.
St. Michael-at-the-North-Gate (St. Michael's Church), 122.
St. Paul's Church, 116.
St. Peter-in-the-East Church, 51.
St. Peter's College, 119.
St. Stephen's House, 132.
St. Thomas the Martyr's Church, 118.
Science Library, The Radcliffe, 138.
Sheldonian Theatre, 85.
Somerville College, 125.

Taylor Institution (Taylorian), 109.
Tennis court, 38.
Trinity College, 96.

Union Society, The Oxford, 121.
University College, 55.
University Museum, 137.
University Press (Clarendon Press), 114.

Wadham College, 78.
Wolfson College, 147.
Worcester College, 111.
Wycliffe Hall, 132.

Zoology Laboratory, 142.

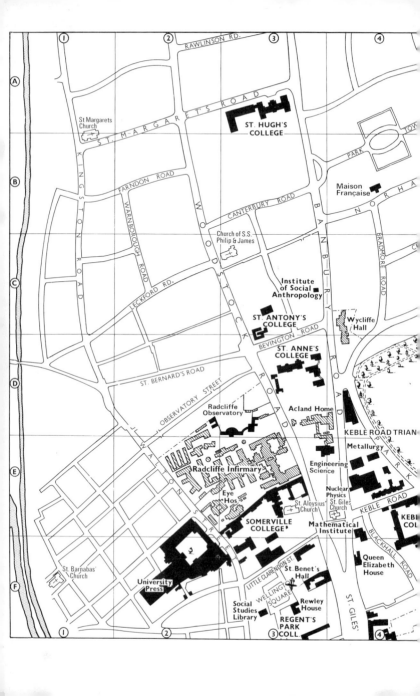

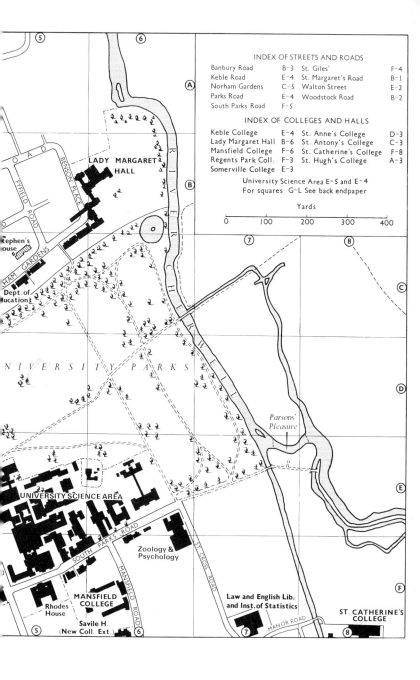

INDEX OF STREETS AND ROADS

Banbury Road	B-3	St. Giles'	F-4
Keble Road	E-4	St. Margaret's Road	B-1
Norham Gardens	C-5	Walton Street	E-2
Parks Road	E-4	Woodstock Road	B-2
South Parks Road	F-5		

INDEX OF COLLEGES AND HALLS

Keble College	E-4	St. Anne's College	D-3
Lady Margaret Hall	B-6	St. Antony's College	C-3
Mansfield College	F-6	St. Catherine's College	F-8
Regents Park Coll.	F-3	St. Hugh's College	A-3
Somerville College	E-3		

University Science Area E-5 and E-4
For squares G-L See back endpaper

Yards

| 0 | 100 | 200 | 300 | 400 |

LADY MARGARET HALL

BENSON PLACE

FYFIELD ROAD

tephen's ouse

Dept. of ucation

R I V E R   C H E R W E L L

U N I V E R S I T Y   P A R K S

Parsons' Pleasure

UNIVERSITY SCIENCE AREA

SOUTH PARKS ROAD

Zoology & Psychology

MANSFIELD ROAD

ST. CROSS ROAD

Law and English Lib. and Inst. of Statistics

MANOR ROAD

Rhodes House

MANSFIELD COLLEGE

Savile H. (New Coll. Ext.)

ST. CATHERINE'S COLLEGE